PETER
GRANSER

CONEY
ISLAND

With an essay by / Mit einem Essay von
Vicki Goldberg

PETER GRANSER

CONEY ISLAND

HATJE
CANTZ

CONTENTS

FOREWORD

Nostalgia and photography are closely related. Every depictive photograph shows us an image of a moment from the past that is hardly distinguishable from a once visible reality. This illusion of the visual presence of historical events, from which photography derives its nostalgic character, may offer an explanation for the fascinating appeal of the Coney Island motif. Coney Island was built as a setting for short-lived sensory amusements, and as such is an embodiment of transience. Decades of exposure to the forces of aging and decline have inscribed the complementary aspects of joy and melancholy into this primal image of the amusement park. Maintaining the same delicate balance between sensitivity and curiosity that typifies his other projects, Peter Ganser has captured the essence of this place where times and cultures merge in striking photographs. The photographer has achieved dense images that transcend the realm of the documentary and serve as metaphors for the condition of Western societies and the people who live in them today.

The Kunsthalle Tübingen is presenting the first large-scale presentation of *Coney Island* within the scope of the exhibition *Peter Granser. Fotoserien 2000–2005*. I would like to thank everyone who contributed to the success of this project, in particular the artist and his gallerists, Jörg Walz, 14-1 Galerie, and Kamel Mennour, Galerie Mennour, as well as Hatje Cantz for producing this fine volume of photographs.

Martin Hellmold
Kunsthalle Tübingen

Das Nostalgische ist dem Fotografischen eng verbunden. Jede aufs Abbildhafte zielende Fotografie zeigt uns den Abzug eines vergangenen Augenblicks, der einer unmittelbar augenfälligen Wirklichkeit zum Verwechseln ähnlich ist. Dieser Schein einer optischen Gegenwart des Historischen, der den nostalgischen Charakter des Fotografischen ausmacht, mag eine Erklärung für den besonderen Reiz liefern, der dem Motiv Coney Island innewohnt. Es wurde erschaffen als ein Ort der flüchtigen sinnlichen Amüsements, denen zugleich die Kehrseite der Vergänglichkeit anhaftet. In dieses Urbild des Vergnügungsparks hat sich infolge langjährigen Verfalls jenes Gegensatzpaar von Lust und Traurigkeit eingeschrieben, das mit dem nostalgischen Prinzip der Fotografie einhergeht. Mit einer Balance zwischen Sensibilität und Neugierde, die auch seine anderen Projekte auszeichnet, hat Peter Granser diesen Ort, an dem sich Zeiten und Kulturen überlagern, in pointierten Bildern festgehalten. Dem Fotografen gelingen visuelle Verdichtungen, die über ein dokumentarisches Interesse hinaus als Metaphern betrachtet werden können für den Zustand westlich geprägter Gesellschaften und der darin lebenden Menschen.

In der Ausstellung *Peter Granser. Fotoserien 2000–2005* wird *Coney Island* in der Kunsthalle Tübingen erstmals in großem Umfang gezeigt. Ich danke allen Beteiligten, besonders dem Künstler und seinen Galeristen Jörg Walz, 14-1 Galerie, und Kamel Mennour, Galerie Mennour, für ihr großes Engagement bei der Umsetzung dieses Projektes sowie dem Hatje Cantz Verlag für die gleichzeitige Realisierung des Fotobuchs.

Martin Hellmold
Kunsthalle Tübingen

THE DEMOCRATIC PARADISE

Once upon a time, in the first decades of the twentieth century, Coney Island was a democratic paradise where rich and poor alike doffed their clothes and immersed themselves in continuous pleasures of the flesh, the eyes, and the city-dweller's lust for thrills. A summertime heaven on earth, a middle- and working-class utopia year round, a mechanical Promised Land, it was a safe and sociable public space that cost a good deal less to get into than the usual kind of heaven. Luna Park, opened in 1903, advertised itself as an "electric Eden,"[1] and if it was not entirely innocent, it was certifiably electric. At night, Luna glittered like a galaxy with a quarter of a million light bulbs, the largest number of electric bulbs ever to grace one site,[2] all of them outlining a sprawling fantasy architecture of arches and towers, turrets and cupolas, and domes.

Coney Island was unique, and its fame reached around the world. Sigmund Freud came to see it, and so did Maxim Gorky. Gorky was so enchanted with the night-time wonderland that he wrote of its "shapely towers and miraculous castles, palaces, and temples…. Fabulous and beyond conceiving, ineffably beautiful is this fiery scintillation."[3] During the day, camels wandered through Luna's grounds, horses dived into pools, and elephants slid down a Shoot the Chutes. In Steeplechase Park, which had opened in 1897, customers raced on mechanical horses. Dreamland, which opened in 1904, offered simulated submarine rides, simulated plane rides (less than a year after the Wright brothers flew for the first time for twelve seconds), and a Fighting the Flames show, with a reported 4,000 people putting out a fire in a six-storey building.[4] All three parks had "fun houses" and fast rides that forced couples to hold on to each other, a rare opportunity at the time.[5] At Steeplechase, costumed performers wandered about, and customers could rent clown suits to wear over their own clothes.[6]

And that is not even to mention the beaches, where rich and poor alike could play in the surf, bask in the sun, and ogle the opposite sex. In 1909, the parts of Coney Island that were extravagant, exotic, otherworldly, and devoted exclusively to pleasures unavailable in daily life were visited by more than twenty million men, women, and children, a larger percentage of the population of the time than the combined number of visitors to Disney's Orlando and Anaheim amusement parks in 1989.[7]

This lavish success was partially due to technological advances. By the turn of the century, electricity not only turned the parks into fairylands, but also lit the city streets, making it safer and more inviting to go out at night, and powered the trolleys that trundled people to the island easily and cheaply. Coney Island's very existence sang the promise of technology, loudly suggesting that mechanical advances would make the world more beautiful, offer new thrills and spectacles, and open the gates to all the delights of leisure. The timing was right: society's addiction to spectacle had been building throughout the nineteenth century, with dioramas, lantern projections, world's fairs, and the advent of the cinema. The public was more than ready for heavy doses of artificial wonders and thrills and frights.

Besides, cities, New York City in particular, were large and crowded, and workdays and work weeks were long and taxing. Factory- and office-bound men and women were in bad need of a break that would take them far from their daily grind, in recognition of which a few of them were even getting unpaid vacations by this time, and some of those were spending their vacations in the city. Coney Island was the most enchanting, accessible, and explicit expression of the new leisure society, which decreed that sun and sea were good for you and recreation something like a necessity—in 1907, the Yiddish *Tageblatt* prodded its immigrant readers to join the parade to pleasure: "He who can enjoy and does not enjoy commits a sin."[8] The industrial revolution, the leisure society, and the culture of the spectacle merged in grand style on Coney Island.

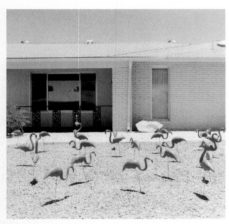

Sun City, *Frontgarden 03*,
2000

Vor langer, langer Zeit, in den ersten Jahrzehnten des zwanzigsten Jahrhunderts, war Coney Island einmal ein demokratisches Paradies, in dem Arm und Reich ihre Kleider abwarfen und sich ununterbrochen den Freuden des Fleisches, der Sinne und der Lust des Städters am Nervenkitzel hingaben. Im Sommer war es der Himmel auf Erden und das ganze Jahr hindurch ein Utopia für Mittel- und Arbeiterklasse, ein mechanisches Gelobtes Land – ein sicherer, geselliger öffentlicher Raum, zu dem sich die Tore für einen weit geringeren Preis öffneten als die Pforten zum Himmel. Der 1903 eröffnete Luna Park pries sich als ein »elektrisches Eden«[1] an, und wenn dieses Eden auch nicht ganz frei von Sünde war, so war es doch eindeutig elektrisch. Nachts glitzerte Luna mit einer viertel Million Glühbirnen wie eine ganze Galaxie – die größte Anzahl von Glühbirnen, die jemals einen Ort geschmückt hat –,[2] und alle diese Lichter zeichneten die Konturen einer wuchernden Fantasiearchitektur mit Bögen und Kuppeln, Türmen und Türmchen nach.

Coney Island war einzigartig, und sein Ruhm verbreitete sich bis ans andere Ende der Welt. Sigmund Freud kam, um es zu sehen, ebenso wie Maxim Gorki. Gorki war so verzaubert von dem nächtlichen Wunderland, dass er von dessen »schönen Türmen und wundersamen Schlössern, Palästen und Tempeln« schrieb: »Märchenhaft und unvorstellbar, unbeschreiblich schön ist dieses feurige Funkeln.«[3] Am Tage wanderten Kamele durch den Luna Park, Pferde tauchten in Schwimmbecken, und Elefanten rutschten eine Wasserbahn hinab. Im Steeplechase Park, der 1897 eröffnet worden war, konnten die Besucher Rennen auf mechanischen Pferden bestreiten. Das 1904 eröffnete Dreamland wartete mit simulierten U-Boot-Fahrten auf, mit Flugsimulatoren (nicht einmal ein Jahr nachdem den Brüdern Wright ein zwölf Sekunden langer Flug gelungen war) und einer Show namens »Kampf gegen die Flammen«, bei der laut zeitgenössischen Angaben viertausend Personen einen Brand in einem sechsstöckigen Gebäude löschten.[4] In allen drei Vergnügungsparks gab es »fun houses« mit Spiegelkabinetten und sich bewegenden Böden sowie schnelle Fahrgeschäfte, die Paare zwangen, sich aneinander festzuklammern, was damals eine seltene Gelegenheit war.[5] Durch den Steeplechase Park schlenderten kostümierte Darsteller, und auch die Besucher konnten Clownanzüge leihen, die sie dann über der eigenen Kleidung trugen.[6]

Und zu alledem gab es ja noch die Strände, wo Arm und Reich sich ohne Unterschied in der Brandung tummeln, in der Sonne liegen und dem anderen Geschlecht schöne Augen machen konnten. Im Jahr 1909 wurden jene fantastischen, exotischen, überirdischen Teile von Coney Island, die ausschließlich solchen Freuden gewidmet waren, wie sie der Alltag nicht bot, von mehr als zwanzig Millionen Männern, Frauen und Kindern besucht – ein größerer Prozentsatz der damaligen Bevölkerung als die Besucherzahlen, die 1989 von den beiden Disney Parks in Orlando und Anaheim zusammen erreicht wurden.[7]

Dieser ungeheure Erfolg war zum Teil dem technischen Fortschritt zu verdanken. Seit der Jahrhundertwende verwandelte die Elektrizität nicht nur die Vergnügungsparks in eine Märchenwelt, sondern erleuchtete auch die Straßen der Stadt, die dadurch sicherer wurden und eher zum Ausgehen einluden, und trieb die Straßenbahnen an, mit denen die Leute problemlos und billig auf die Insel kamen. Coney Islands ganze Existenz sang ein Loblied auf die Technik und propagierte lautstark die Ansicht, dass mechanische Neuerungen die Welt schöner machen, für neue Attraktionen und Sensationen sorgen und die Schleusen für alle Wonnen der Freizeit öffnen würden. Es war der richtige Zeitpunkt: Dioramen, Laterna-magica-Projektionen, Weltausstellungen und die Anfänge des Kinos hatten im neunzehnten Jahrhundert die Sucht der Gesellschaft nach dem Spektakel beständig zunehmen lassen. Die Öffentlichkeit war mehr als bereit für eine starke Dosis von künstlichen Wundern, Attraktionen und Schrecken.

Zudem waren die Städte, besonders New York, groß und quollen über vor Menschen, und der Arbeitstag und die Arbeitswoche waren lang und strapaziös. Die an das Fließband und den Schreibtisch gefesselten Männer und Frauen hatten eine Erholungspause bitter nötig, und zwar eine, die sie weit von der täglichen Schinderei forttrug. In Anerkennung dieser Tatsache bekamen manche von ihnen zu dieser Zeit sogar unbezahlten Urlaub, und einige verbrachten diesen Urlaub in der Stadt. Coney Island war der reizvollste, am leichtesten erreichbare und unverhüllteste Ausdruck der neuen Freizeitgesellschaft, die verfügte, dass Sonne und Meer gut für den Menschen waren und Erholung so etwas wie eine Notwendigkeit. So spornte etwa das jiddische *Tageblatt* seine Leser, vor allem Einwanderer, im Jahr 1907 an, sich der Parade des Vergnügens anzuschließen: »Wer sich erfreuen kann und es nicht tut, der begeht eine Sünde.«[8] Die industrielle Revolution, die Freizeitgesellschaft und die Kultur des Spektakels gingen auf Coney Island eine grandiose Verbindung ein.

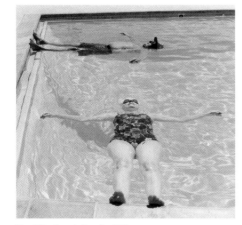

Sun City, *Couple in a Pool 02,*
2000

The Democratic Paradise
Vicki Goldberg

The merger had a long life and naturally enough changed greatly over the course of it. The parks flourished through the 1920s, and even during the Depression of the 1930s their gates remained open: they touted cheaper attractions like sideshows and strip joints, lured huge crowds to the beaches and picnic grounds, and hotdogs (invented on the island and made famous by Nathan's Famous, open since 1916) cost only a nickel and fed a multitude. After World War II, the amusement parks and beaches exerted a stronger pull than ever on a populace with money in its pocket and a need to make up for lost time. Trouble started in the 1960s, when an urban renewal program demolished many houses, apartment buildings, and landmarks to make space for large housing projects, effectively destroying the existing community on the island. America was at last passing laws mandating desegregation, and an influx of blacks, both as residents and visitors, prompted many whites to move and white parents to keep their children away out of fear.[9] By the 1970s, Coney Island had a new reputation, this time for blight. The housing projects were a shambles; the area had become a home to prostitutes and was riddled with crime.

By the time Peter Granser came to check out the place it had reached a peculiar juncture. Efforts were already under way to renew the island. The housing projects had begun to be cleaned up, and by 2001 a ballpark would rise where the roller coaster once zoomed around Steeplechase Park and hidden vents in a theater blew ladies' skirts up without notice. The Parachute Jump (known as the "Eiffel Tower of Brooklyn"), the Wonder Wheel, and the Cyclone have all been declared landmarks, and a few mechanical rides still operate.[10] The beaches continue their siren call in summertime, though they are no longer a destination for the wealthy as they were in the early days, when luxury hotels lined one end of the island. The place no longer reeks of crime. Russian immigrants have established a lively community on the island. There is a good supply of desolation—the democratic paradise is decidedly scruffy—but there is life in the old place yet. Peter Granser trained his camera on a Coney Island in transition.

The island's American dream of technologically engineered leisure and spectacle looks slightly forlorn through his lens, which registers a mix of sweet smiles and emptiness, dry humor and melancholy that he refers to as its "wonderful morbid charm." To the extent that technology has relocated the dream of spectacular leisure to films, TV, video-game parlors, and the Internet, the newer artificial reality is not exactly what the early Coney Island seemed to promise. Though there are still crowds on the beaches, Granser focuses more often on nearly abandoned stretches of sand; and though families and couples do come to play beside the swoop of roller coaster tracks, isolation visits the beaches and the boardwalk. Boardwalk strollers walk in solitude, single figures dot vast and lonesome beaches, an old lady slumps exhausted before pictures of sprightly sea horses, trash accumulates like an alien colony preparing to take over. If you know anything about the history of Coney Island (and the history of the eternally optimistic American dream), these photographs quietly comment on social change and on the character of today, which yesterday inevitably turns into.

Coney Island was from the beginning so quintessentially American that Granser's photographs of its twenty-first century existence still represent aspects of the American way of life. An offbeat way of life, perhaps, where past and present, dream and reality brush elbows, and sunlight and ice-cream cones merge with chain-link fences and garbage. Granser, an Austrian citizen who lives in Germany, has a keen eye for the exaggerations and absurdities that decorate the edges of American popular culture and of constructed lives in general. Born in 1971 and self-taught as a photographer, he began his career as a press reporter, moved on to personal documentary, and in 1997 began to work in color, starting with *Sun City* (published 2003), a book about the first American city built solely as a retirement community. In *Sun City's* carefully tended, aseptically clean community, a manicured haven blessed by Arizona's steady sun, Granser took precise note of people's dime-store attempts at establishing their individuality and reinventing their environment. There are plaster deer on their gravel lawns, dancing frogs and flamingos among Seguaros as big as King Kong, and interiors and exteriors so pristine that the air has been sucked out of them and replaced with light, which becomes a volume in itself. One photograph of bored, elderly women seeking glamour under hairdryers is followed by a picture of metal canes hung up on a wall in orderly profusion: a reminder of the bravado of all human efforts to beautify life.

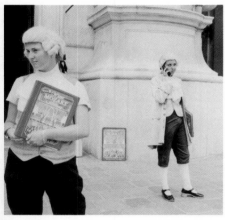

**Austria, *Mozart 01,*
2002**

Dieser Verbindung war ein langes Leben beschieden, in dessen Verlauf sie sich naturgemäß gewaltig veränderte. Die Vergnügungsparks florierten die gesamten zwanziger Jahre hindurch, und selbst während der Wirtschaftskrise der Dreißiger blieben ihre Tore geöffnet: Sie warben mit billigeren Attraktionen wie Monstrositätenshows und Stripteaselokalen, lockten gewaltige Menschenmassen an die Strände und auf die Picknickplätze, und Hotdogs (die auf der Insel erfunden und durch den Schnellimbiss »Nathan's Famous«, den es seit 1916 gibt, berühmt wurden) kosteten nur fünf Cent und machten die Massen satt. Nach dem Zweiten Weltkrieg übten die Vergnügungsparks und Strände eine noch stärkere Anziehungskraft auf die Bevölkerung aus, die jetzt Geld in der Tasche hatte und das Bedürfnis, die verlorene Zeit wettzumachen.

Die Probleme begannen in den sechziger Jahren, als im Zuge eines Stadterneuerungsprogramms viele Häuser, Wohnblöcke und Wahrzeichen abgerissen wurden, um Platz zu schaffen für große soziale Wohnungsbauprojekte, wodurch das bestehende soziale Gefüge der Insel zerstört wurde. Amerika verabschiedete endlich Gesetze, die eine Aufhebung der Rassentrennung anordneten, und der Zustrom von Schwarzen – als Einwohner wie als Besucher – veranlasste viele Weiße, fortzuziehen, und weiße Eltern, ihre Kinder von der Insel fernzuhalten.[9] So hatte Coney Island in den Siebzigern schließlich eine neue Berühmtheit erlangt, diesmal als heruntergekommene Gegend. Die Wohnblocks waren völlig verfallen, Prostituierte hatten sich in der Gegend niedergelassen, und die Insel war eine Hochburg des Verbrechens.

Als Peter Granser nach Coney Island kam, um sich dort umzusehen, stand die Insel gleichsam am Scheideweg. Bemühungen um ihre Sanierung waren bereits im Gang. Man hatte damit begonnen, die Wohnblocks aufzuräumen, und bis zum Jahr 2001 sollte dort, wo einst die Achterbahn durch den Steeplechase Park raste und versteckte Ventilatoren den Damen ohne Vorwarnung die Röcke hochbliesen, ein Baseball-Stadion entstehen. Der Parachute Jump (der Fallschirmsprungturm, der als der »Eiffelturm von Brooklyn« bekannt ist), das Wonder-Wheel-Riesenrad und die Cyclone-Achterbahn wurden unter Denkmalschutz gestellt, und einige dieser Fahrgeschäfte sind noch in Betrieb.[10] Der Reiz, der von den Stränden im Sommer ausgeht, ist ungebrochen, auch wenn die Reichen nicht mehr dorthin fahren, wie einst, als das eine Ende der Insel von Luxushotels gesäumt war. Es riecht auf der Insel nicht mehr nach Verbrechen. Russische Einwanderer haben ein lebendiges Viertel aufgebaut. Es gibt immer noch genug Elend – das demokratische Paradies ist eindeutig schmuddelig –, aber die gute alte Insel ist noch voller Leben. Peter Granser richtete seine Kamera auf ein Coney Island im Übergang.

Durch seine Kamera gesehen, die eine Mischung aus reizendem Lächeln und Leere, trockenem Humor und Melancholie registriert – er selbst nennt dies den »wunderbaren morbiden Charme« von Coney Island –, wirkt der amerikanische Traum der Insel von einer technisch gesteuerten Freizeit und Spektakelkultur ein wenig verloren. Da die Technik den Traum von einer spektakulären Freizeit auf Film, Fernsehen, Videospielhallen und das Internet übertragen hat, ist die neue künstliche Realität nicht gerade das, was das frühe Coney Island zu versprechen schien. Obwohl die Strände immer noch voll sind, richtet Granser den Blick häufiger auf nahezu verlassene Sandstreifen, und obwohl durchaus Familien und Paare auf die Insel kommen, um sich neben den steilen Achterbahngleisen dem Spiel zu ergeben, breitet sich an den Stränden und auf der Promenade Einsamkeit aus. Menschen schlendern allein die Promenade entlang, breite, einsame Strände sind gesprenkelt mit vereinzelten Gestalten, eine alte Dame sitzt zusammengesackt vor Bildern von munteren Seepferdchen, Müll sammelt sich wie eine Kolonie von Außerirdischen, die sich bereitmachen zur Machtübernahme. Wenn man die Geschichte von Coney Island kennt (und die Geschichte des amerikanischen Traums mit seinem ewigen Optimismus), bilden diese Fotografien einen stillen Kommentar zu den gesellschaftlichen Veränderungen und zum Charakter der Gegenwart, zu der die Vergangenheit unweigerlich wird.

Coney Island war von Anfang an so durch und durch amerikanisch, dass Gransers Fotografien von dessen Erscheinungsbild im einundzwanzigsten Jahrhundert immer noch Aspekte des amerikanischen Lebensstils zeigen. Ein ausgefallener Lebensstil vielleicht, in dem Vergangenheit und Gegenwart, Traum und Realität sich miteinander verbrüdern und Sonnenschein und Eiswaffeln sich mit Gitterzäunen und Müll vereinigen. Granser, der als österreichischer Staatsbürger in Deutschland lebt, hat einen scharfen Blick für die Übertreibungen und Absurditäten, die die Peripherie der amerikanischen Populärkultur zieren, und für jede Art von konstruiertem Leben. 1971 geboren und als Fotograf ein Autodidakt, begann er seine Karriere als Fotojournalist, ging dann zu freien, persönlichen Fotoprojekten über und fing 1997 an, in Farbe zu arbeiten, beginnend mit *Sun City* (erschienen 2003), einem Buch über die erste amerikanische Stadt, die als reine Rentnersiedlung gebaut wurde. In dieser adretten, bis zur Keimfreiheit sauberen Kleinstadt in Arizona, einem gepflegten, von der Sonne verwöhnten Zufluchtsort, zeichnete Granser genauestens die Versuche der Leute auf, mithilfe von Massenprodukten ihre Individualität zu behaupten und ihre Umgebung zu gestalten. Man sieht Plastikhirsche auf Rasenflächen aus Kies, tanzende Frösche und Flamingos zwischen Kakteen, so groß wie King Kong, und Innen- und Außenräume von einer solchen Unberührtheit, dass es scheint, als wäre alle Luft aus ihnen abgesogen und durch Licht ersetzt worden, das zu einem eigenen Volumen wird. Einer Aufnahme von gelangweilten, alten Damen, die sich unter Trockenhauben um Glamour bemühen, folgt ein Bild von Gehhilfen, die in wohl geordneter Fülle an der Wand hängen: ein Verweis auf die gespielte Tapferkeit, die in allen menschlichen Versuchen steckt, das Leben schöner zu machen.

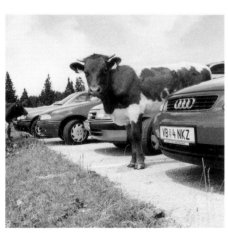

Austria, *Cows,*
2002

In Austria, Granser photographed another society hovering between different eras and realities under an onslaught of leisure—a country overrun by tourists looking for picturesque tradition. The overlap of the actual and the wished for looks like theater: a cow parked between cars in a parking lot, a person dressed like Mozart speaking on a cell phone, a cut-out of an officer on guard by a highway. Granser has also photographed Germans who dress up as cowboys in a land that does not have any, and Elvis devotees who slick back their hair and stuff their middle-aged spreads into jeweled white jumpsuits in imitation of the King. Even Granser's book on Alzheimer's patients in a center in Stuttgart, a series of photographs that scrupulously manage to preserve the dignity of people who have apparently already lost it, deals with the construction of identity by focusing on the results of its dissolution.

Granser allows his subjects a modicum of dignity, though they may seem silly, undeservedly pretentious, sad, even outrageous to a casual observer. His photographs take people on their own terms—and on our own terms, we humans prefer to think we are worth presenting to the world. Standing at a middle distance, both physically and emotionally, he maintains a lingering degree of the kind of neutrality that Walker Evans thought he could accomplish by refusing to treat his subjects like objects. Granser is wholly aware that the pride and imagination of certain people are as tacky and incongruous as the perplexing culture they maneuver in, but his comments, sometimes made by way of wry pairs of pictures, are delivered with calm irony, like a remark made by someone with a subtle sense of humor who changes neither his tone nor his facial expression.

Humor was not considered much of an art form while photography was struggling to be taken seriously as art, but work by such photographers as Jacques-Henri Lartigue, Elliott Erwitt, and Robert Doisneau raised its standing. Granser has said that after he met Martin Parr in 1997, he switched from black and white to color,[11] and surely Parr had the further effect of encouraging the younger man to look at the droll side of the leisure and products of a consumer society in order to plumb its foibles, desires, and incongruities, and to pick up clues to the fuel it runs on. Granser's pictures of Coney Island may strike you as a series of straightforward, entertaining, nostalgic, and sad reports on a particular place, but they add up to an account of America's determined and persistent pursuit of pleasure, the hodge-podge of classes engaged in the hunt (though there is no one from the yacht-club set here), and the unrelenting tendency of loneliness and alienation to raise their heads in the midst of good times.

Martin Parr sets a highly subversive standard for this kind of social reporting. He works at being at least as preposterous, jazzy, and kitsch as his subject matter, and he comes in as close as an unarmed assault. His color is honky-tonk; his laughter, of which there is plenty, is a guffaw. Granser's is a milder temperament. His stance is diffident, his amusement discreet, his color for the most part as reticent as his distance, which is invariably polite. The beaches and boardwalks in his pictures tend to be bleached by the sun, though when the amusement park's brilliant turquoise and yellow and chartreuse make their demands for attention, he gives them their due. Granser does not appear to interfere overtly with what is before the lens except to say "May I take your picture?" He does not alter or rearrange people or things except to occasionally place them in front of a fitting background. He does not seem to impose his opinion, but simply to declare that he is an observer and you may make of the scene what you will. His opinion—a better word might be attitude—is all in the choice of subject, the angle of approach, the decisions on what to include or exclude.

There is no such thing as a truly neutral photograph or one without a viewpoint and a judgment, except perhaps those taken mechanically in a particle accelerator or an orbiting telescope, but on a photographic spectrum of close and distant, hot and cool, judgmental and impartial, Granser is obviously closer to the slightly removed attitude of two photographers he admires, Stephen Shore and William Eggleston. Then too, he shares their loyalty to the unspectacular and less-noticed facets of everyday life. His photographs rely not on drama, but on the rewards of a steady gaze and a respectful insistence on looking hard. His tranquil contemplation at its best uncovers the exceptional squirreled away in the mundane, quirks of color, unexpected geometries, an occasional unpredictable incident lurking in a corner, plus the humorous comment that a companion image offhandedly supplies.

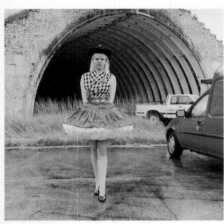

German Cowboys, *Cowgirl,*
2002

In Österreich fotografierte Granser eine Gesellschaft, die, von einer Freizeitwelle überrollt, zwischen verschiedenen Zeitaltern und Realitäten schwebt – ein Land, in das Touristenhorden einfallen, die auf der Suche nach malerischem Brauchtum sind. Die Überschneidung zwischen dem Tatsächlichen und dem Ersehnten sieht wie Theater aus: eine Kuh, die zwischen Autos geparkt ist, eine Person in Mozarttracht, die mit dem Handy telefoniert, ein Papp-Polizist, der an einer Landstraße wacht. Granser hat auch Deutsche fotografiert, die sich in einem Land, in dem es keine Cowboys gibt, als solche verkleiden, und Elvis-Fans, die sich in Nachahmung des Kings das angeklatschte Haar zurückkämmen und ihren Wohlstandsspeck in mit Glassteinen besetzte weiße Overalls zwängen. Gransers Buch über Alzheimer-Patienten in einem Stuttgarter Zentrum zeigt eine Serie von Fotografien, denen es auf gewissenhafte Weise gelingt, die Würde von Menschen zu bewahren, die diese schon verloren zu haben scheinen. Selbst hier behandelt Granser das Thema der Konstruktion von Identität, indem er den Blick auf die Folgen ihrer Auflösung richtet.

In seinen Projekten lässt er den Menschen, die er fotografiert, immer einen Funken Würde, so albern, unfreiwillig angeberisch, traurig, ja haarsträubend sie uns auf den ersten Blick erscheinen mögen. Seine Fotografien nehmen die Menschen so, wie sie sind. Denn wir Menschen glauben nun einmal gerne, dass wir es wert sind, der Welt gezeigt zu werden. Dadurch dass Granser eine gewisse Distanz zu ihnen hält, sowohl körperlich als auch emotional, bewahrt er ein bestimmtes Maß von jener Art Neutralität, die Walker Evans glaubte erreichen zu können, indem er sich weigerte, die von ihm fotografierten Menschen wie Objekte zu behandeln. Dass der Stolz und die Fantasie gewisser Leute so geschmacklos und ungereimt sind wie die verwirrende Kultur, in der sie agieren, ist Granser sehr wohl bewusst. Doch seine Kommentare, die zum Teil durch pointierte Paarungen von Bildern entstehen, entbehren nicht einer gelassenen Ironie – als würde jemand mit einem feinen Sinn für Humor eine Bemerkung machen, ohne dass sich sein Ton oder sein Gesichtsausdruck verändern.

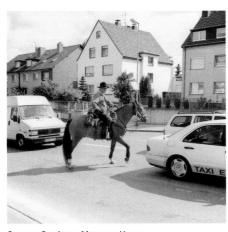

German Cowboys, *Man on a Horse,*
2002

Als die Fotografie noch darum kämpfte, als Kunst ernst genommen zu werden, galt Humor kaum als künstlerisches Mittel, aber die Werke von Fotografen wie Jacques-Henri Lartigue, Elliott Erwitt und Robert Doisneau verhalfen ihm zu mehr Ansehen. Granser erklärte, dass er, nachdem er 1997 Martin Parr kennen gelernt hatte, von Schwarz-Weiß zu Farbe übergegangen sei.[11] Darüber hinaus hatte diese Begegnung zweifellos den Effekt, dass der Jüngere sich ermuntert sah, seinen Blick auf die komische Seite der Freizeit und der Produkte der Konsumgesellschaft zu richten, um ihre Schwächen, Sehnsüchte und Ungereimtheiten auszuloten und Hinweise darauf zu sammeln, was diese Gesellschaft in Gang hält. Gransers Bilder von Coney Island mögen wie ein geradliniger, unterhaltsamer, nostalgischer und trauriger Bericht über einen bestimmten Ort wirken. Aber zusammengenommen zeigen sie Amerikas entschlossene, hartnäckige Jagd nach dem Vergnügen, das Kunterbunt der daran beteiligten Schichten (auch wenn die Gruppe der Yachtbesitzer hier nicht vertreten ist) sowie die unbarmherzige Neigung von Einsamkeit und Entfremdung, sich mitten im schönsten Vergnügen bemerkbar zu machen.

Martin Parr hat für diese Art von Sozialreport einen höchst subversiven Standard gesetzt. Er arbeitet daran, mindestens ebenso haarsträubend, poppig und kitschig zu sein wie sein Gegenstand, und er rückt ihnen dabei bedrohlich dicht auf den Leib. Seine Farben sind billig und grell, sein Gelächter, an dem es nicht mangelt, ist schallend. Granser hat ein sanfteres Naturell. Seine Einstellung ist eher zurückhaltend, seine Belustigung diskret, seine Farben sind größtenteils so unaufdringlich, wie er selbst es ist in dem höflichen Abstand, den er stets wahrt. Die Strände und Promenaden auf seinen Bildern sind meist von der Sonne gebleicht, obwohl Granser, wenn das leuchtende Türkis, Gelb und Hellgrün der Vergnügungsparks nach Beachtung schreien, ihnen diese durchaus zukommen lässt. Er scheint auf das, was ihm vor die Linse kommt, keinen offenkundigen Einfluss zu nehmen, außer dass er fragt: »Darf ich Sie fotografieren?« Er verändert nichts an den Personen und Dingen, stellt sie höchstens vor einen passenden Hintergrund, scheint niemandem seine Ansicht aufzudrängen, sondern einfach zu erklären, dass er ein Beobachter ist und man aus der Szene machen kann, was man will. Seine Ansicht – oder vielleicht sollte man es lieber Einstellung nennen – zeigt sich nur in der Wahl des Sujets, der Art, wie er es angeht, der Entscheidung, was mit aufs Bild kommt und was nicht.

Natürlich gibt es keine wirklich neutrale Fotografie, das heißt keine, die frei von jedem Standpunkt und Urteil ist – außer vielleicht die mechanischen Aufnahmen aus einem Teilchenbeschleuniger oder einem die Erde umkreisenden Teleskop. Aber in einem fotografischen Spektrum von nah bis fern, heiß bis kalt, wertend bis unparteiisch bewegt sich Granser eindeutig in der Nähe der leicht distanzierten Haltung zweier Fotografen, die er sehr schätzt: Stephen Shore und William Eggleston. Mit ihnen hat er zudem die Treue zu den unspektakulären und weniger beachteten Seiten des Alltags gemein. Seine Fotografien setzen nicht auf das Drama, sondern auf die Früchte eines unbeirrbaren Blicks und des respektvollen Beharrens darauf, ganz genau hinzusehen. In seinen Arbeiten deckt sein ruhiger kontemplativer Blick das Außergewöhnliche auf, das im Prosaischen verborgen liegt, eigentümliche Ausbrüche von Farbigkeit, unerwartete Geometrien, manchmal auch ein unvorhersehbares Ereignis, das in einer Ecke lauert – und das alles mit dem humorvollen Kommentar, den ein daneben gestelltes Bild gleichsam beiläufig abgibt.

His human subjects are sometimes happy and proud, but even when better described as peculiar do not think themselves so or are comfortable as they are. Everyone on earth who can afford it is in costume as himself or herself, presenting an image to the world. At Coney Island, the artifice is sometimes highly evident, though swimmers have less protective cover. Several ludicrously garbed mermaids, on their way to a parade, pose with good cheer and self-possession by fenced-off parking lots uninhabitable by mermaids, or just by fences, which apparently sprout faster than grass on Coney Island. A gray-bearded, tattooed muscleman shows off gargantuan biceps and a gargantuan cod piece. A person who is probably but unconvincingly a man and who wears a transparent but unrevealing garment is located opposite a picture of two bare-chested men and a bare-chested boy. A trio of hipsters with cameras about their necks, in front of a wall full of loopy graffiti and the word "punk," dare us to contemplate their cool, while on the opposite page a clean geometrical abstraction of closed stores seen on the diagonal shelters a rather elegantly drawn advertisement for hotdogs, chips, and pop.

Words and objects play at riposte too. A U.S. Army Recruiting Station that has imposed itself on the façade of Nathan's faces a picture of a young couple (the woman has a Nathan's soda in her hand) who stand before a wall that says "NO." An ad for a judge's program on TV that says "WATCH" in bold letters is paired with a picture of a cop who, well, watches. A nasty scene of teenagers wading through watermelon rinds and plastic is next to a shot of five totally empty wastebaskets. Blow-up figures of mighty Spiderman and Batman flanking, of all creatures, Tweetie, stand opposite a picture of a store that offers the unalloyed satisfaction of shooting Saddam (or Sadam, depending on which façade you read).

What this adds up to is a culture where the pursuit of happiness is a guarantee as well as a goal that is not always met, where a good time is had by some, and daily life slogs on amid monuments to amusement and artificial dream worlds. If a man is known by the company he keeps, a society may be known by the pleasures it seeks.

Artists and photographers have had their eyes on Coney Island for over a century, aware that it was both a spectacle and a metaphor. From early times it was, in fact, a national icon and an emblem of New York—a symbol of national ingenuity and singularity and the country's manifest destiny of "have a good day." Countless photographs, mostly anonymous, advertised the parks' capricious architecture and enticements early in the twentieth century in brochures and journals and on postcards. Art photographers were not yet flocking there, but painters did come.

It seems that just about everyone who has made images of Coney Island found there what he or she was looking for. In part that means that they took their styles with them, and their predilections; in part it means that Coney's very essence was so large a compound of imagination, ambition, consumerism, and aspiration that it was open to myriad interpretations. In the early part of the century, the painter Reginald Marsh went to the beach and limned a tangle of muscular bodies that look like nothing so much as a battle scene by Pollaiuolo. Joseph Stella went there and painted a dynamic abstraction of lights, spotlights, speed, thrust, loops, jagged forms and shards of color, and the whole frenzied potential of technology.

Elvis Tribute Artists, *Hand,*
2004

Die Menschen, die er fotografiert, sind zum Teil glücklich und stolz, aber selbst wenn man sie eher als absonderlich beschreiben würde, halten sie sich nicht dafür oder fühlen sich wohl, so wie sie sind. Jeder von uns, der es sich leisten kann, ist als er selbst verkleidet und präsentiert der Welt ein Bild. In Coney Island ist dieser Kunstgriff manchmal deutlich zu sehen, auch wenn Badende nicht so viel haben, was sie bedeckt und schützt. Einige grotesk gekleidete Meerjungfrauen, die auf dem Weg zu einer Parade sind, posieren frohgemut und selbstbeherrscht vor eingezäunten Parkplätzen, die völlig ungeeignet sind für ihresgleichen, oder einfach vor Zäunen, die auf Coney Island anscheinend schneller aus dem Boden schießen als Gras. Ein graubärtiger, tätowierter Muskelmann stellt stolz seinen enormen Bizeps und seine pralle Hose zur Schau. Einer Person, die wahrscheinlich ein Mann ist, wenn auch auf wenig überzeugende Weise, und die ein transparentes Kleidungsstück trägt, durch das man doch nichts sieht, steht ein Bild von zwei Männern und einem Jungen mit nackten Oberkörpern gegenüber. Drei japanische »Hipster« mit Kameras um den Hals vor einer Wand, die mit verschlungenen Graffiti und dem Wort »punk« besprüht ist, fordern uns auf, uns doch anzusehen, wie cool sie sind. Auf dem Bild daneben verdeckt die saubere geometrische Abstraktion geschlossener Geschäfte in Schrägansicht eine eher elegant gemalte Werbung für Hotdogs, Pommes frites und Cola.

Auch Wörter und Gegenstände können eine schlagfertige Antwort geben. Einer Rekrutierungsstation der US-Armee, die sich vor die Fassade von Nathan's gedrängt hat, ist das Bild eines jungen Paares gegenübergestellt (die Frau hält ein Getränk von Nathan's in der Hand), das vor einer Wand mit einem aufgesprühten »no« steht. Ein Plakat, das für die Fernsehsendung eines Richters wirbt und den Betrachter in fetten Buchstaben auffordert: »watch«, steht neben der Aufnahme eines Polizisten, der dasteht und – wacht. Ein unappetitliches Bild von Teenagern, die durch Schalen von Wassermelonen und Plastikmüll waten, bildet ein Paar mit einer Aufnahme von fünf völlig leeren Papierkörben. Den beiden aufblasbaren Figuren der sagenhaften Helden Spiderman und Batman, die ausgerechnet Tweetie flankieren, steht das Bild eines Ladens gegenüber, der seinen Kunden das ungetrübte Vergnügen verspricht, auf Saddam schießen zu dürfen (oder Sadam, je nachdem, welche der Fassaden man liest).

Insgesamt ergibt sich daraus eine Kultur, in der das Streben nach Glück einerseits garantiert ist, andererseits ein Ziel, das man nicht immer erreicht, in der manche Menschen Spaß haben und der Alltag sich zwischen Denkmälern für das Vergnügen und künstlichen Traumwelten dahinschleppt. Wenn man den Charakter eines Menschen daran erkennt, was für Freunde er hat, so erkennt man den einer Gesellschaft daran, welchen Vergnügungen sie frönt.

Seit mehr als einem Jahrhundert haben Künstler und Fotografen Coney Island ins Visier genommen, in dem Bewusstsein, dass es sowohl ein Spektakel als auch eine Metapher ist. Tatsächlich war es fast von Anfang an eine nationale Ikone und ein Sinnbild für New York – ein Symbol für die Erfindungskraft und Einzigartigkeit des Landes und dessen greifbare Bestimmung, die darin besteht, »einen schönen Tag« zu haben. Zahllose Fotografien, meist anonymen Ursprungs, warben zu Beginn des zwanzigsten Jahrhunderts auf Postkarten und in Broschüren und Zeitschriften für die ausgefallene Architektur und die Verlockungen der Vergnügungsparks. Künstlerische Fotografen strömten damals noch nicht dorthin, aber die Maler kamen.

Es scheint, dass fast jeder, der Bilder von Coney Island gemacht hat, dort gefunden hat, was er suchte. Das heißt einerseits, dass die Künstler ihren Stil und ihre Vorlieben mitbrachten, andererseits bedeutet es, dass Coney Island von seinem Wesen her ein so umfassendes Gemisch aus Fantasie, Ehrgeiz, Konsum und Sehnsüchten war, dass es sich für unzählige Interpretationen anbot. Zu Beginn des Jahrhunderts ging der Maler Reginald Marsh an den Strand und stellte einen Wust von muskulösen Körpern dar, der große Ähnlichkeit mit einer Schlachtszene von Pollaiuolo hat. Joseph Stella kam und malte in dynamischer Abstraktion Lichter, Scheinwerfer, Geschwindigkeit, Schubkraft, Schleifen, gezackte Formen und Farbsplitter und das ganze wild gewordene Potenzial der Technik.

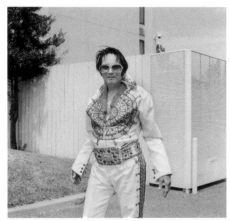

Elvis Tribute Artists, *Elvis Tribute Artist 01,*
2004

The Democratic Paradise
Vicki Goldberg

Coney Island may have been too low-brow for pictorialist photographers, but from about 1930 on, a lot of American photographers traipsed out to its precincts. The 1930s were a high time of documentary photography, and serious photographers continued to prowl the city's nooks and crannies, including the island, long afterward. Walker Evans looked at a couple contemplating the wonderland before them. Weegee, that insatiable eye on New York, went to the beach in 1940 and photographed what looked like half the city's population crammed into one space and watching the birdie as Weegee snapped their portrait. Lisette Model, an immigrant, photographed an exceedingly large lady having an exceedingly joyous wallow in the shallow edge of the ocean. Soon, Sid Grossman came looking for lovers on the beach, Leon Levinstein closed in on epic backs and flesh overwritten by tattoos, Harry Lapow concentrated on the massive forms of arms, knees, and bulky torsos, and Arthur Leipzig snapped the bliss of sunbathing, cuddling, being dashed about on the rides. Bruce Davidson followed a teenage gang there, and Garry Winogrand photographed gamblers and sea creatures that upstaged people.

Some photographers were less sanguine: Robert Frank focused on a fully clothed black man sleeping on the beach far from the festivities; Diane Arbus photographed a couple arguing and a wax woman being strangled by a wax man in the museum. Most of these photographs were taken in the 1950s and 1960s, just before the big decline set in, and all of them were black and white. More recently, Bruce Gilden took black-and-white film to the beaches once more and discovered that the sand was still home to the overweight, the dispirited, and the odd, and Mary Ellen Mark saw a couple of boys looking lost before an empty stretch of sand.

Coney Island in color is less gritty and has a new life redolent of its old one as an invitation to excitement. (Though when Rineke Dijkstra photographed an adolescent on the beach there, in color, she preferred to present a beach as anonymous as the others she frequents.) The deep turquoise Tilt-A-Whirl and the blue extravagance of mermaid hair, the pale pink latex jaws of shark masks, even the pallid beach, gray ocean, and sky speak of how bold the search for entertainment has been and how pale the results sometimes are. Visitors and residents add their delights and discontents, their habitual masquerades and beach personas, their smiles and loneliness and bids for attention to the mechanical caprices, the banquet of junk food, and the theater of signs. If Coney Island stands for a wider America than its little piece of land, perhaps it is closest to the Beat poet Lawrence Ferlinghetti's book *A Coney Island of the Mind*, which the jacket claims is about "a kind of circus of the soul." Granser himself says of Coney Island, "It is sometimes funny, sometimes bizarre, sometimes tragic and sometimes melancholic—just like life itself."

Alzheimer, *Portrait 19*,
2001

1   Richard Snow, *Coney Island:*
    A Postcard Journey to the City of Fire
    (New York, 1984), p. 14, cited in David Nasaw,
    Going Out: The Rise and Fall of
    Public Amusements (New York, 1993), p. 83.

2   Robert E. Snow and David E. Wright,
    "Coney Island: A Case Study in Popular Culture
    and Technical Change," *Journal of Popular*
    Culture 9 (Spring 1976), p. 967, cited in Nasaw
    1993 (see note 1), p. 83.

3   Cited in Charles Denson, *Coney Island:*
    Lost and Found (Berkeley, 2002), p. 31.

4   Nasaw 1993 (see note 1), pp. 83, 85.

5   See ibid., pp. 89/90.

6   See photograph on p. 33 of Denson 2002
    (see note 3).

7   Nasaw 1993 (see note 1), p. 3.

8   Andrew R. Heinze, *Adapting to Abundance:*
    Jewish Immigrants, Mass Consumption,
    and the Search for Identity (New York, 1990),
    p. 130, cited in Nasaw 1993 (see note 1), p. 4.

9   See Denson 2002 (see note 3), p. 105,
    and Nasaw 1993 (see note 1), p. 253.

10 Denson 2002 (see note 3), pp. 131, 123.

11 Félipa de Almeida, "The retro but
    contemporary kitsch of Peter Granser,"
    Sur La Terre (December 2004), pp. 78–81.

Das demokratische Paradies
Vicki Goldberg

Für die Piktorialisten war Coney Island vielleicht zu unkultiviert, aber seit den dreißiger Jahren bummelten viele amerikanische Fotografen durch die dortigen Viertel. Die dreißiger Jahre waren eine Hochzeit der Dokumentarfotografie, und auch lange danach durchstreiften bedeutende Fotografen noch alle Winkel und Ecken der Stadt, die Insel eingeschlossen. Walker Evans richtete seinen Blick auf einen Mann und eine Frau, die zu dem vor ihnen liegenden Wunderland hinüberblickten. Weegee, dieser unersättliche Beobachter des New Yorker Großstadtlebens, ging 1940 an den Strand und fotografierte etwas, das so aussah, als wäre die halbe Einwohnerschaft der Stadt auf einem Fleck zusammengezwängt worden und hielte Ausschau nach dem Vögelchen, während Weegee sie porträtierte. Die Immigrantin Lisette Model nahm eine außerordentlich dicke Frau auf, die sich außerordentlich lustvoll in dem seichten Wasser am Ufer wälzt. Wenig später kam Sid Grossman und suchte am Strand nach Liebespaaren, Leon Levinstein näherte sich Rücken von epischer Breite und mit Tätowierungen voll geschriebenem Fleisch, Harry Lapow konzentrierte sich auf die massigen Formen von Armen, Knien und gewaltigen Torsos, und Arthur Leipzig knipste das Glück, das darin liegt, sich in der Sonne zu aalen, zu schmusen und in den Fahrgeschäften herumgeworfen zu werden. Bruce Davidson folgte einer Gang von Teenagern, und Garry Winogrand fotografierte Spieler und Meerestiere, die den Menschen die Schau stehlen.

Einige Fotografen waren weniger optimistisch: Robert Frank richtete den Blick auf einen voll bekleideten Mann, der weit von den Festivitäten entfernt am Strand schläft. Diane Arbus fotografierte ein sich streitendes Paar und eine Wachsfrau im Museum, die von einem Wachsmann erwürgt wird. Die meisten dieser Fotografien entstanden in den fünfziger und sechziger Jahren, kurz bevor der große Niedergang einsetzte, und sie waren alle schwarzweiß. In neuerer Zeit ist Bruce Gilden wieder mit Schwarz-Weiß-Filmen an die Strände gegangen und hat festgestellt, dass der Sand nach wie vor die Heimat der Übergewichtigen, der Entmutigten und der schrägen Vögel ist, und Mary Ellen Mark sah ein paar Jungen, die vor einem leeren Sandstreifen sehr verloren wirkten.

Coney Island in Farbe ist weniger finster und verfügt über ein neues Leben, das stark an sein altes erinnert, als eine Einladung zu aufregenden Erlebnissen (auch wenn Rineke Dijkstra, als sie dort am Strand einen Teenager fotografierte, es vorzog, einen Strand zu zeigen, der genauso anonym ist wie alle, die sie aufsucht). Das leuchtend türkisfarbene Karussell und das extravagante blaue Meerjungfrauenhaar, der blassrosa Latexrachen der Haimasken, ja selbst der fahle Strand, das graue Meer und der Himmel verraten, wie kühn die Suche nach Unterhaltung war und wie blass zuweilen das Ergebnis ist. Den verrückten Einfällen der Technik, dem Bankett aus Junkfood und dem Theater der Schilder fügen die Besucher und Einwohner ihre eigenen Freuden und Unzufriedenheiten, ihre beständige Maskerade und ihre speziellen Strandpersönlichkeiten, ihr Lächeln und ihre Einsamkeit hinzu. Wenn Coney Island für einen größeren Teil von Amerika steht als für dieses kleine Stück Land, dann entspricht es vielleicht am ehesten dem Buch *A Coney Island of the Mind* des Beat-Poeten Lawrence Ferlinghetti, das laut Klappentext von »einer Art Zirkus der Seele« handelt. Granser selbst sagt über Coney Island: »Es ist mal komisch, mal bizarr, mal tragisch und mal melancholisch – genau wie das Leben.«

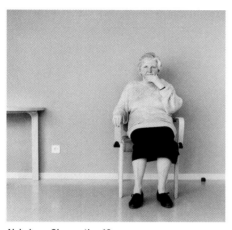

Alzheimer, *Observation 19,*
2001

1   Richard Snow, *Coney Island.*
    A Postcard Journey to the City of Fire,
    New York 1984, S. 14, zit. nach David Nasaw,
    Going Out. The Rise and Fall of
    Public Amusements, New York 1993, S. 83.

2   Robert E. Snow und David E. Wright,
    »Coney Island. A Case Study in Popular Culture
    and Technical Change«, in: *Journal of Popular*
    Culture, 9, Frühjahr 1976, S. 967, zit. nach Nasaw
    1993 (s. Anm. 1), S. 83.

3   Zit. nach Charles Denson, *Coney Island.*
    Lost and Found, Berkeley 2002, S. 31.

4   Nasaw 1993 (s. Anm. 1), S. 83, 85.

5   Ebenda, S. 89 f.

6   Vgl. die Abb. auf S. 33 in Denson 2002
    (s. Anm. 3).

7   Nasaw 1993 (s. Anm. 1), S. 3.

8   Andrew R. Heinze, *Adapting to Abundance.*
    Jewish Immigrants, Mass Consumption,
    and the Search for Identity, New York 1990,
    S. 130, zit. nach Nasaw 1993 (s. Anm. 1), S. 4.

9   Vgl. Denson 2002 (s. Anm. 3), S. 105,
    und Nasaw 1993 (s. Anm. 1), S. 253.

10 Denson 2002 (s. Anm. 3), S. 131, 123.

11 Félipa de Almeida,
    »The retro but contemporary
    kitsch of Peter Granser«,
    in: *Sur La Terre,* Dezember 2004, S. 78–81.

PHOTOGRAPHS

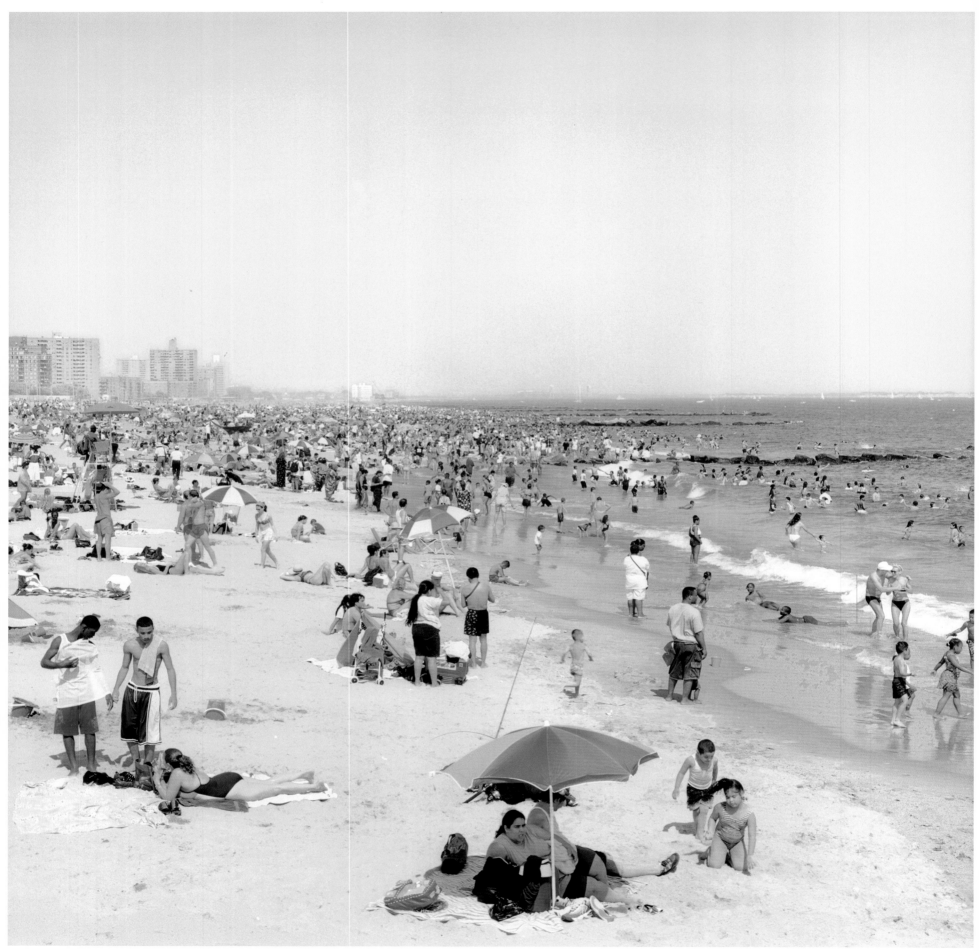

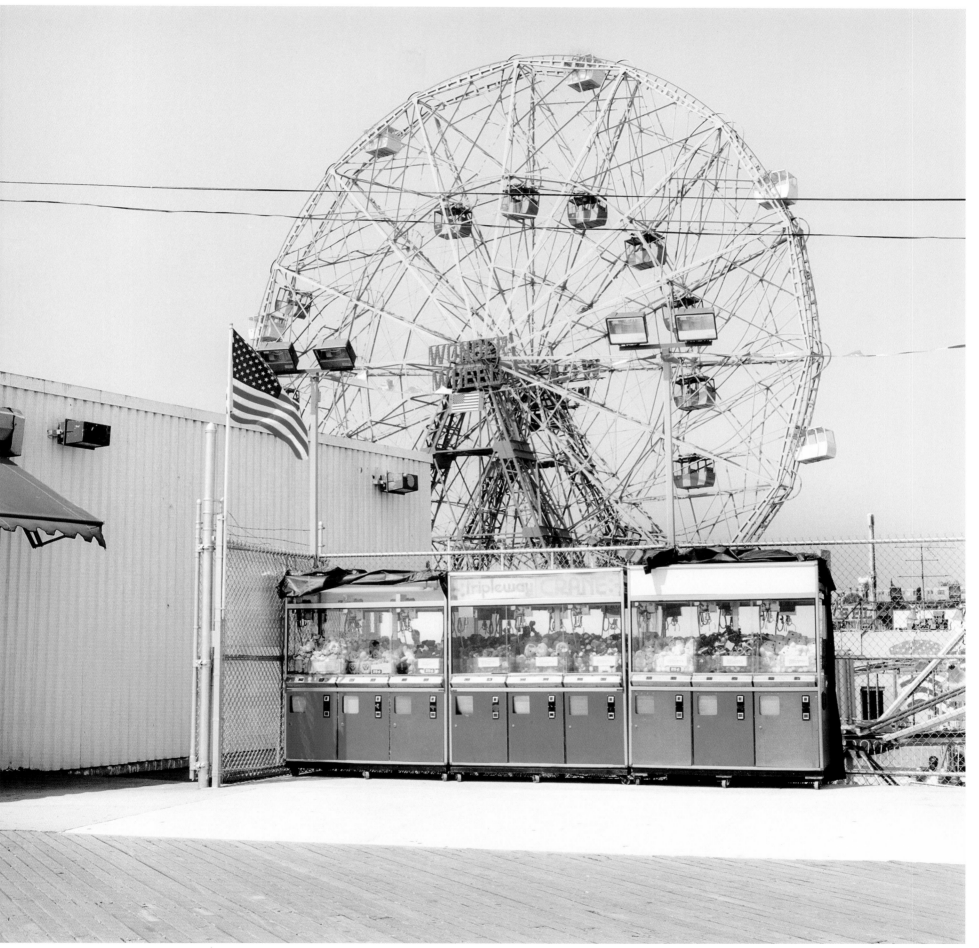

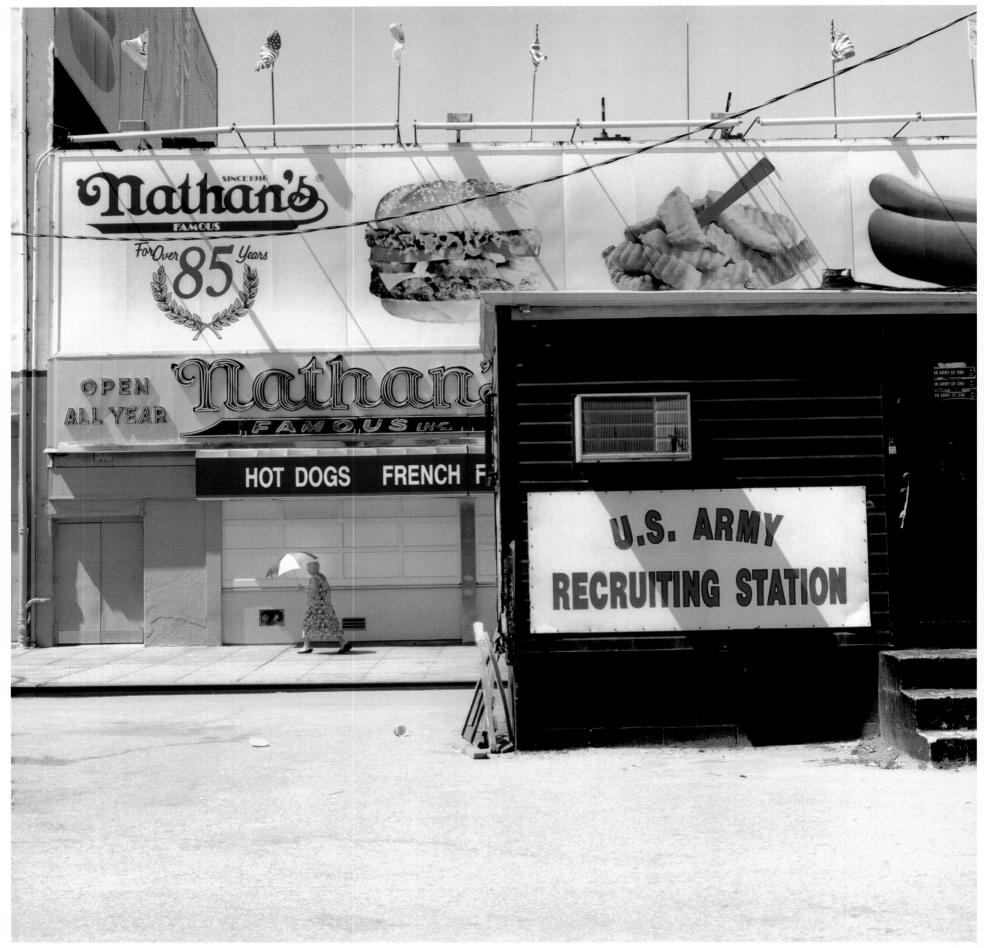

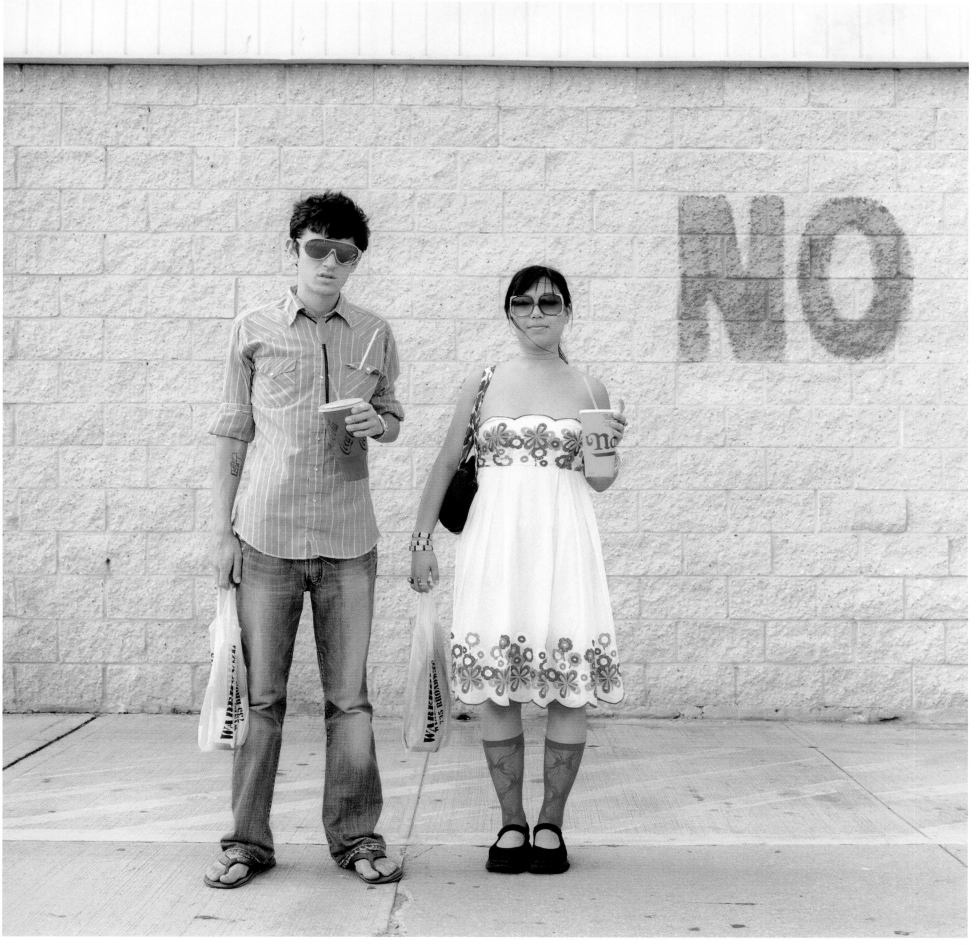

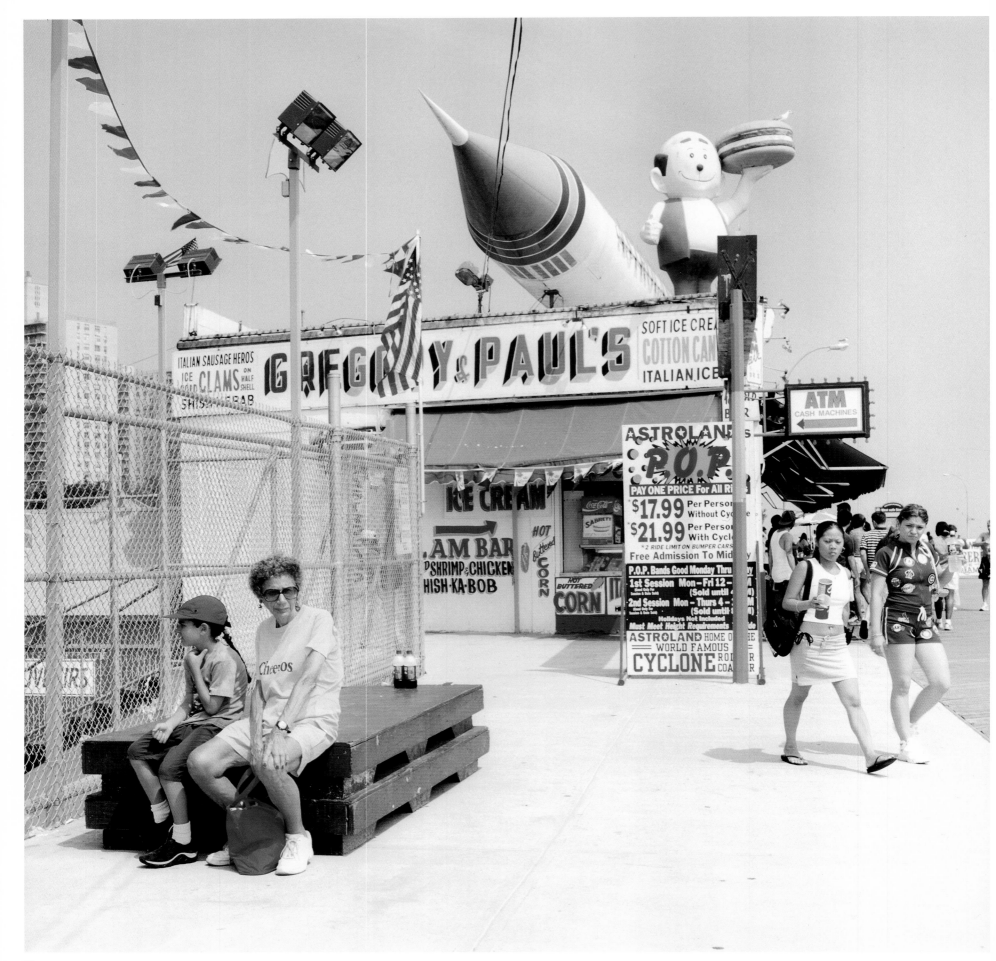

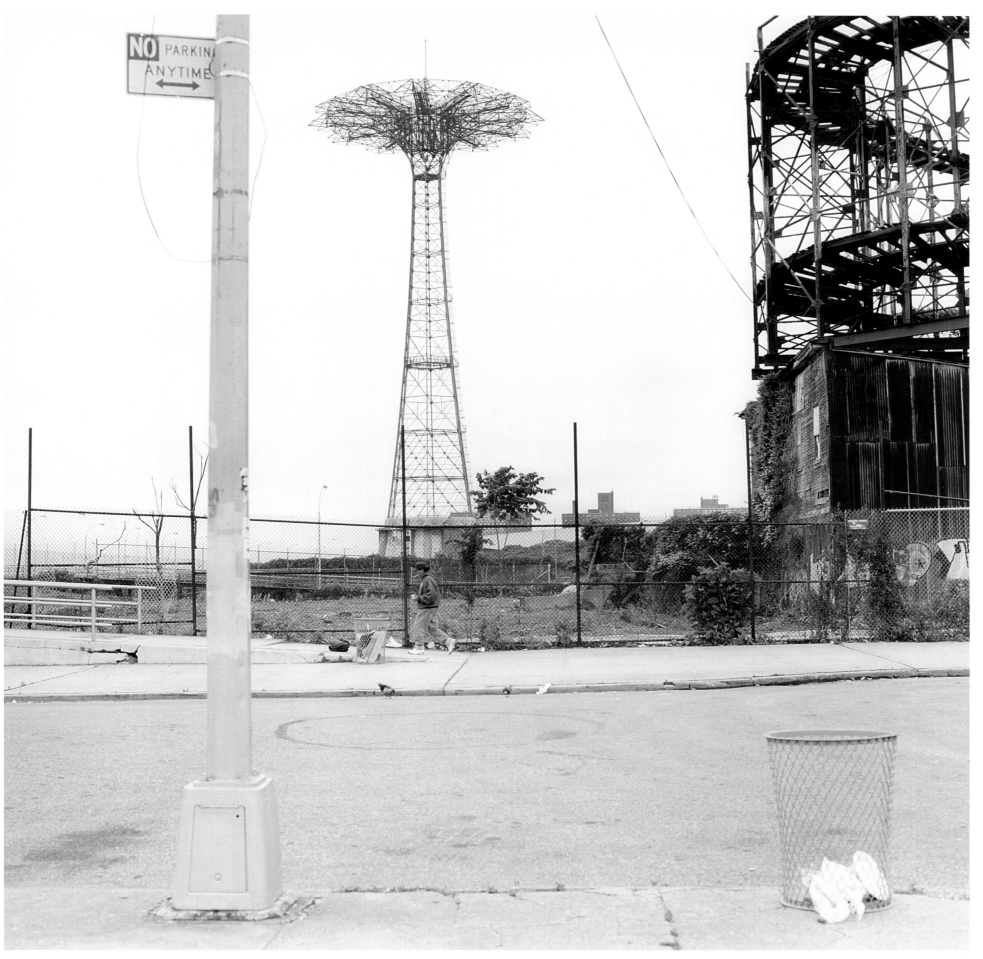

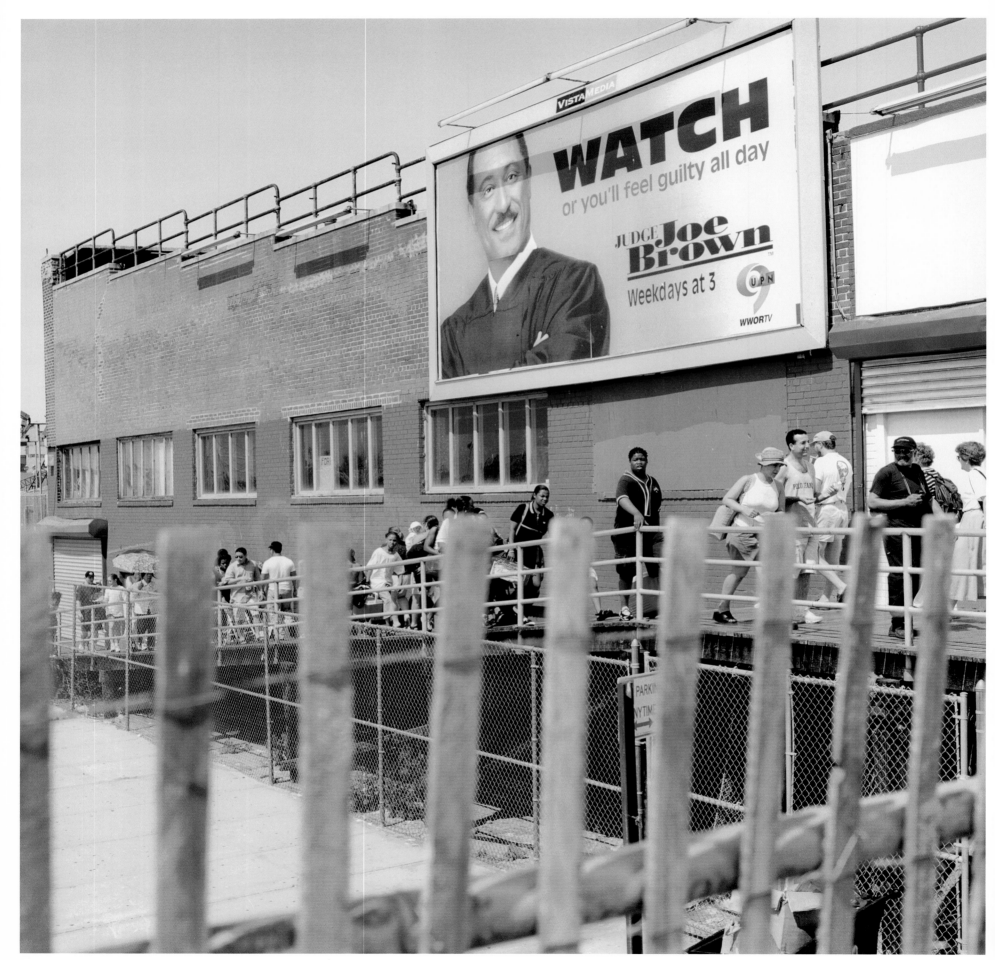

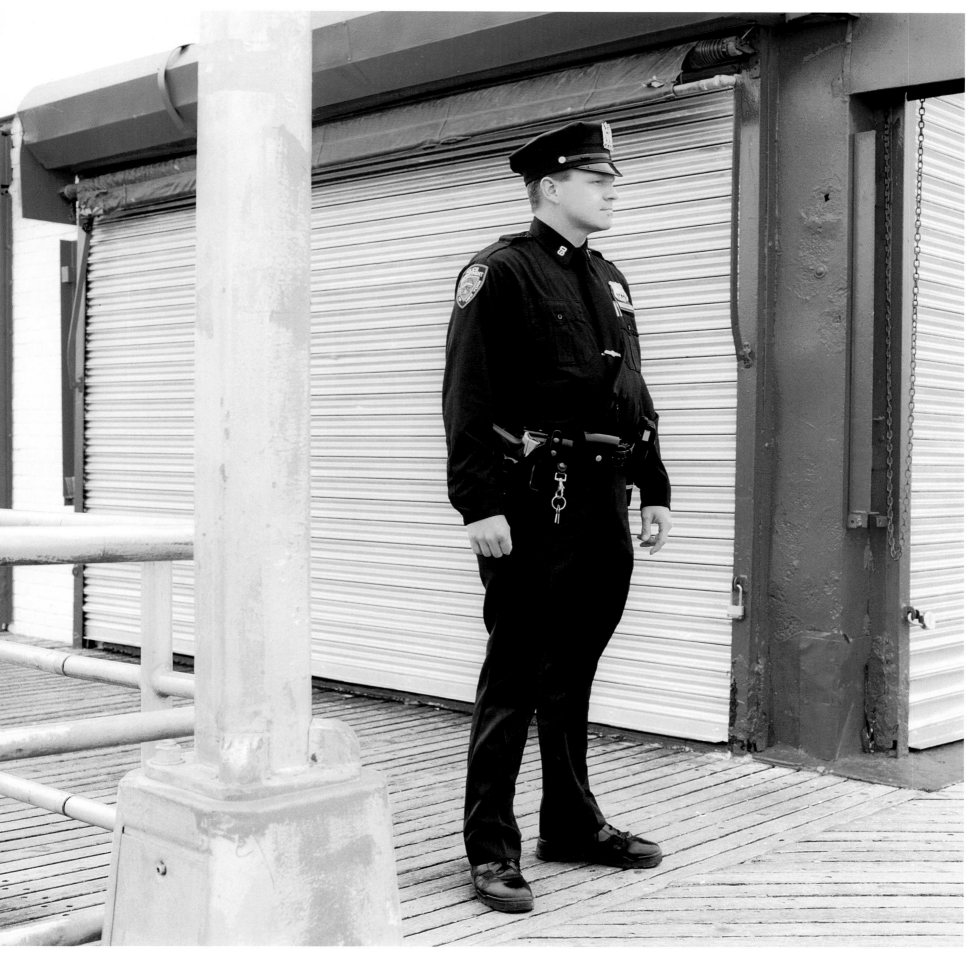

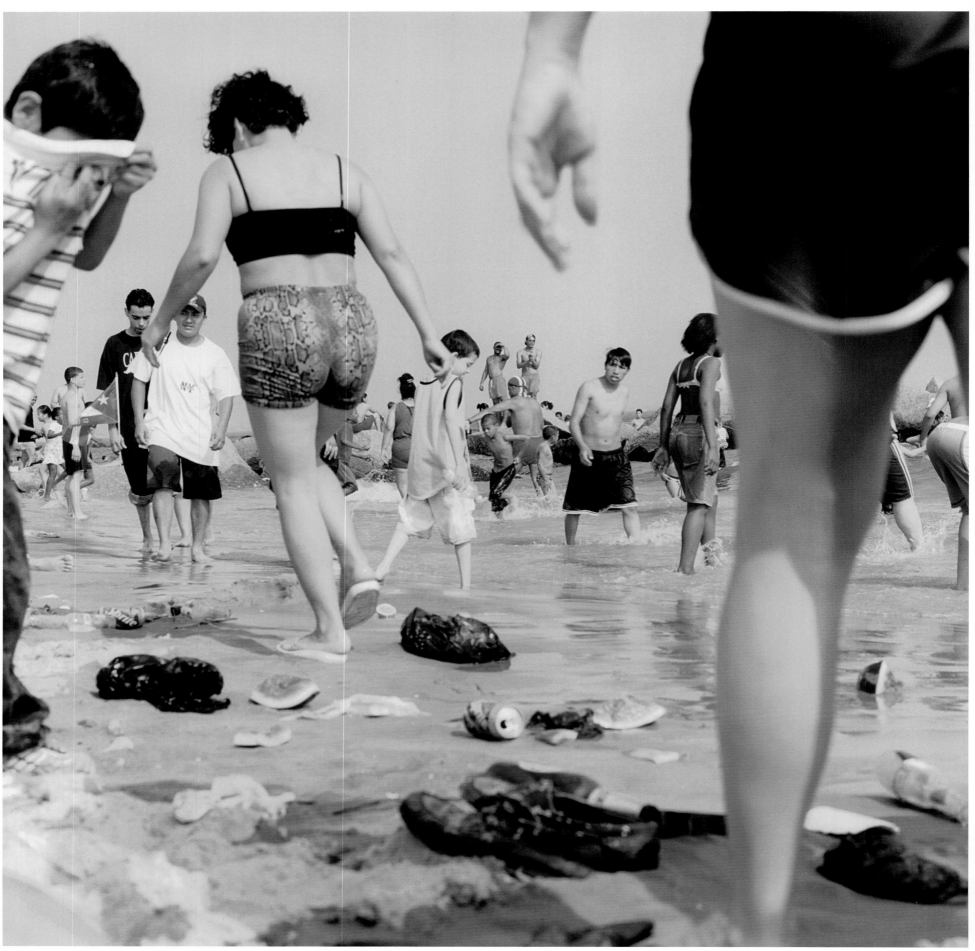

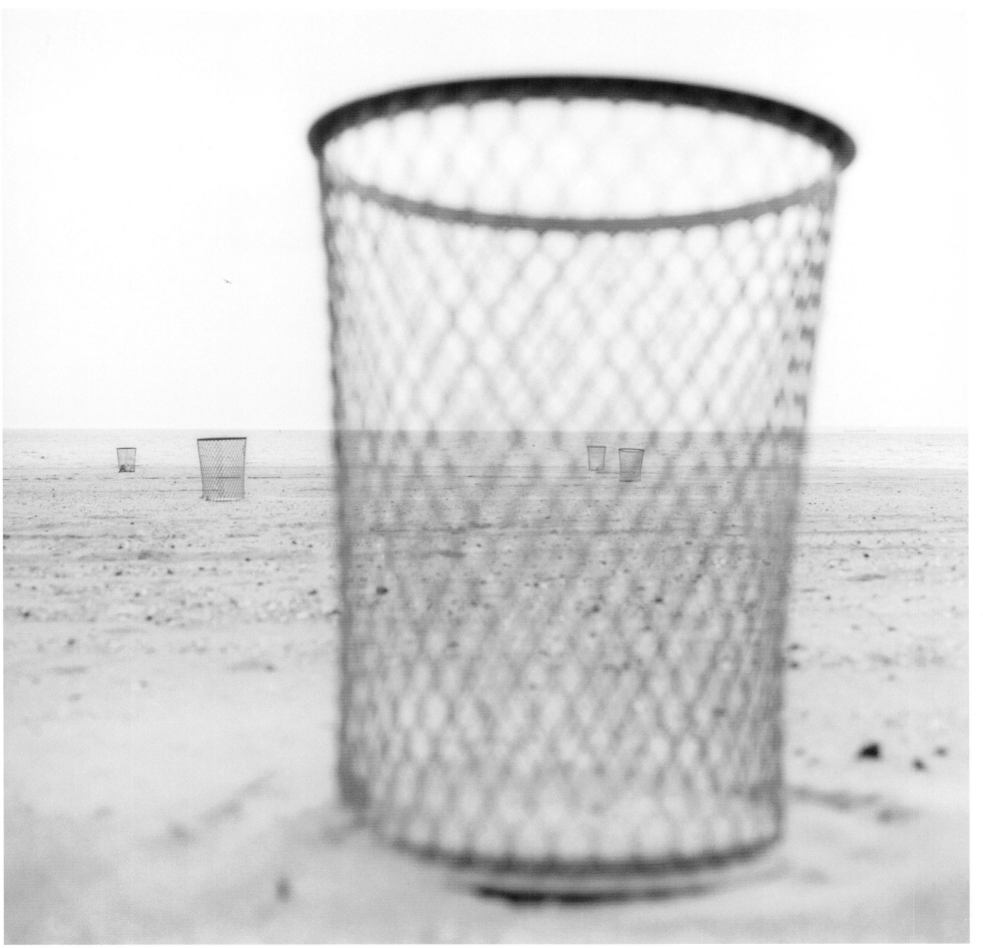

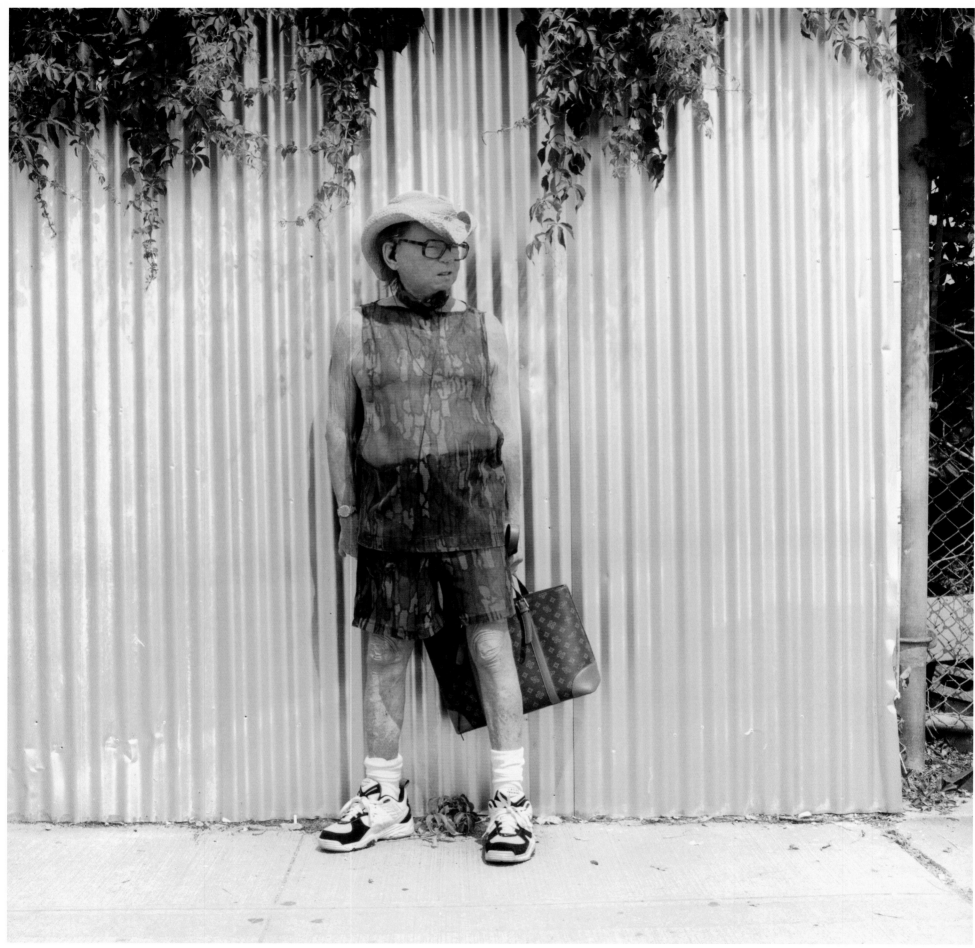

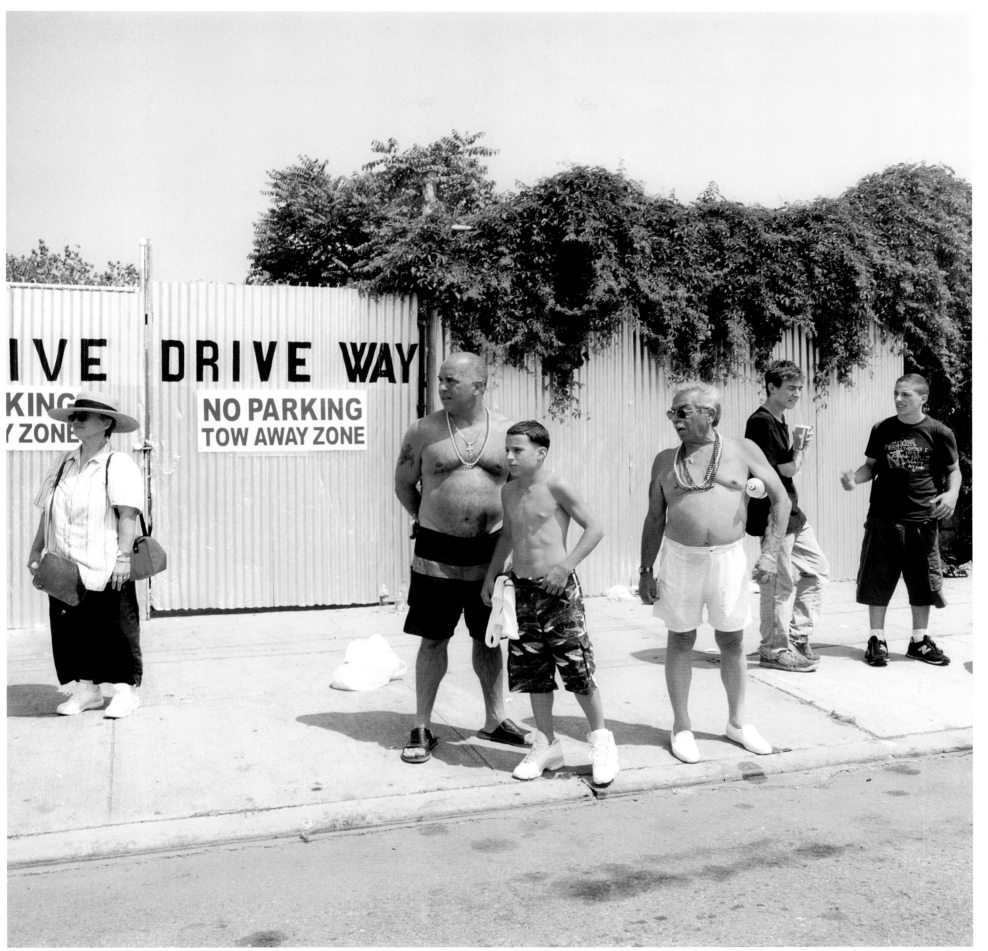

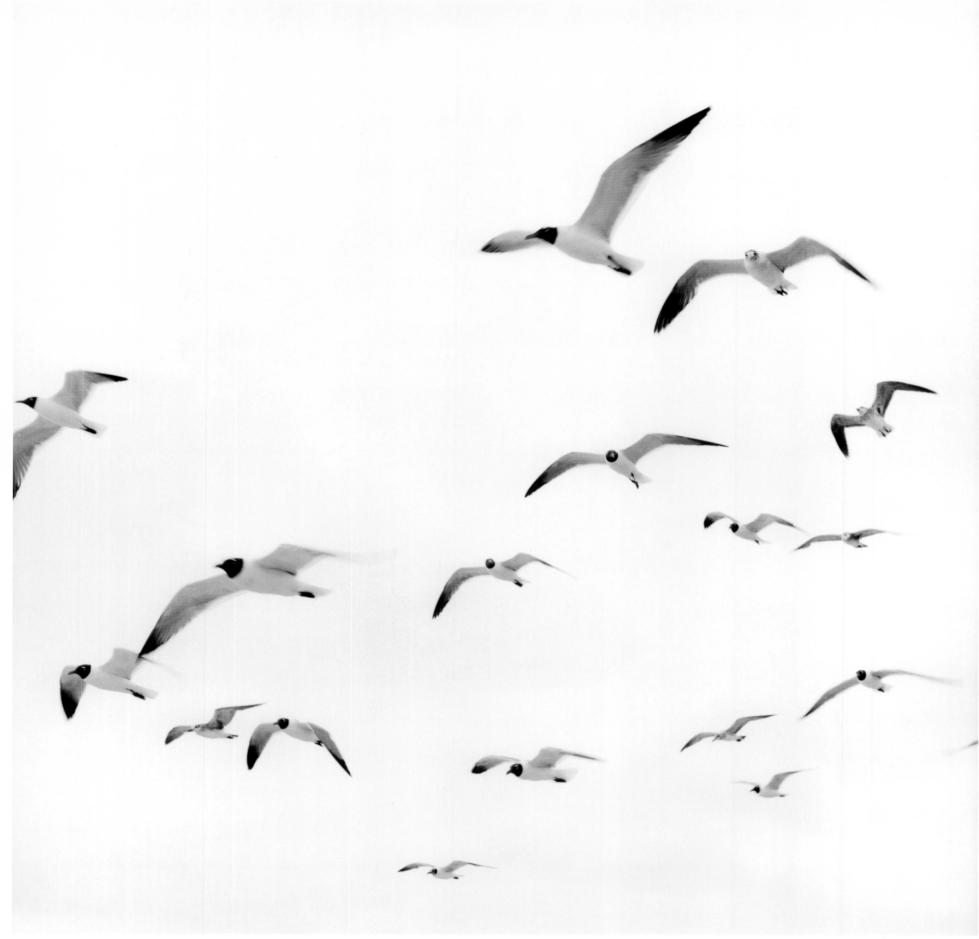

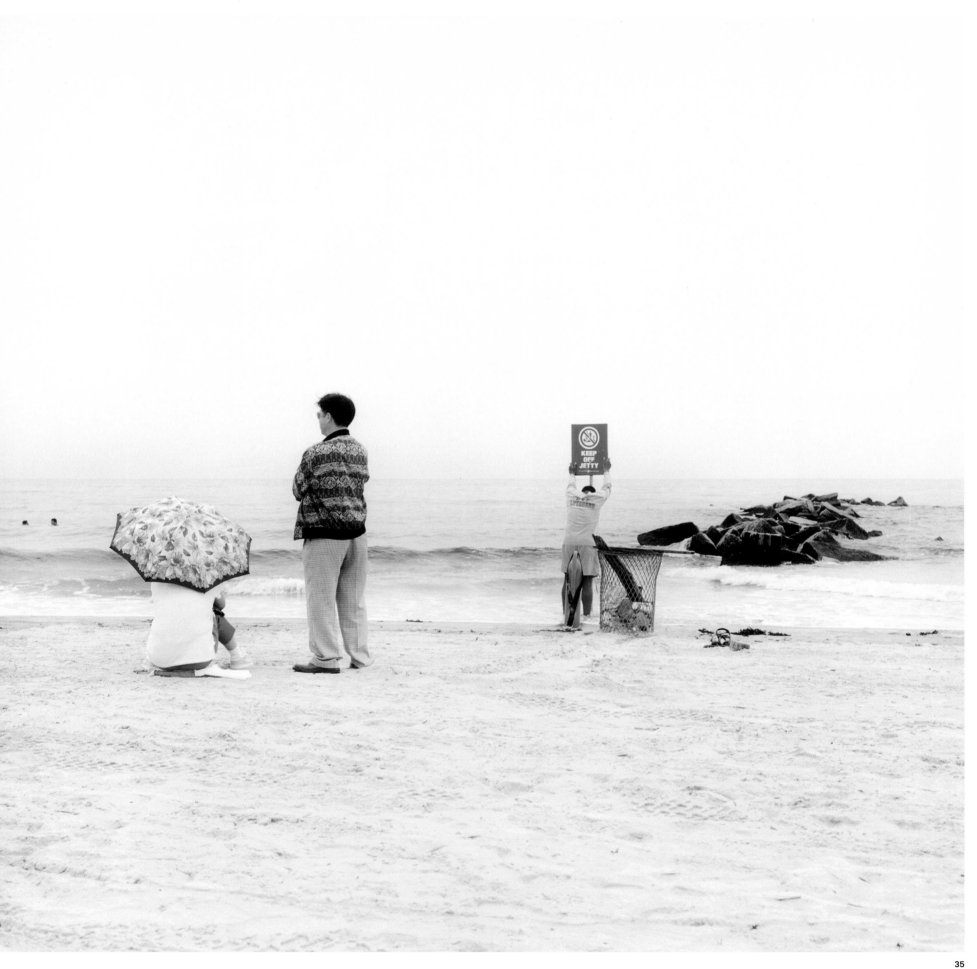

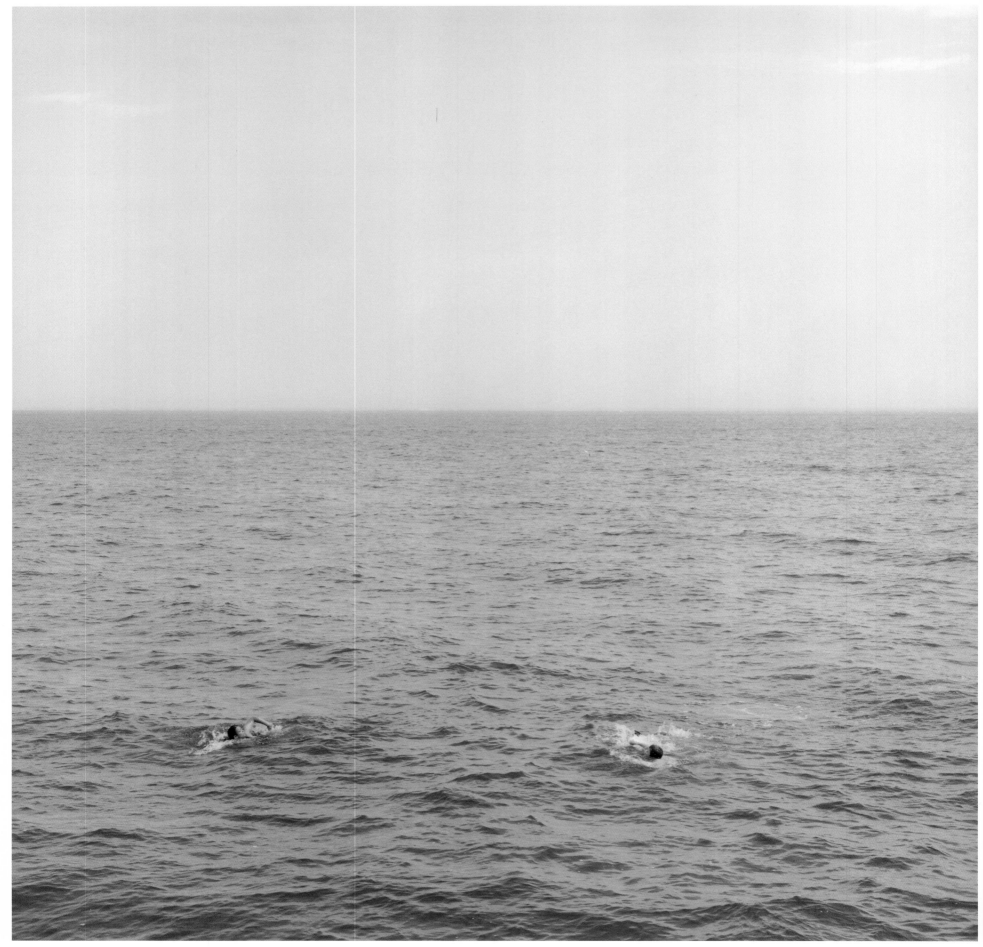

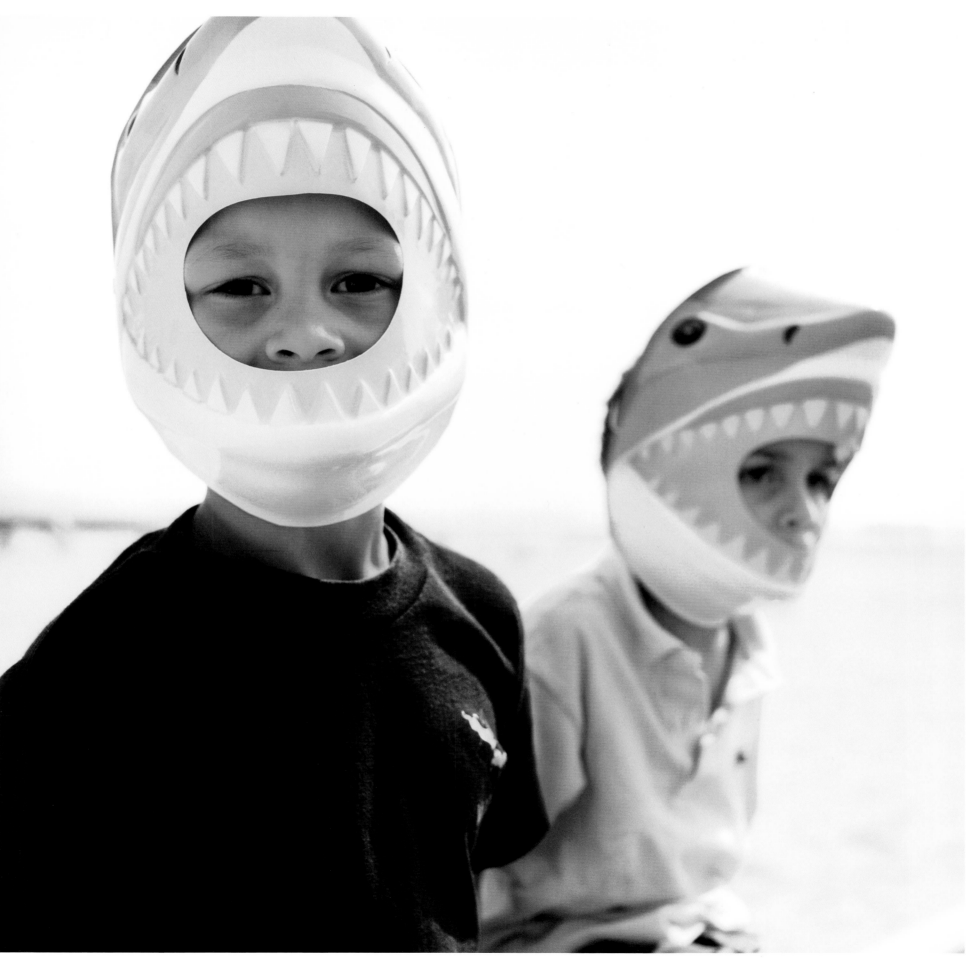

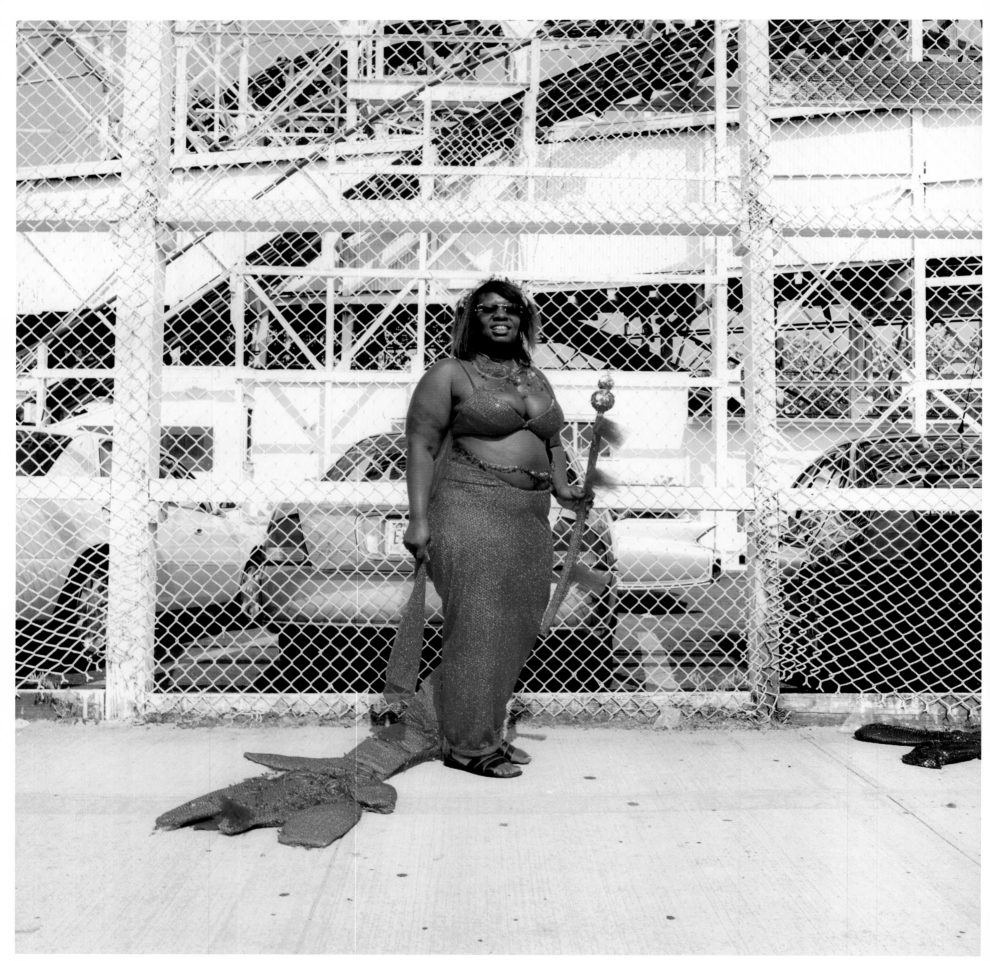

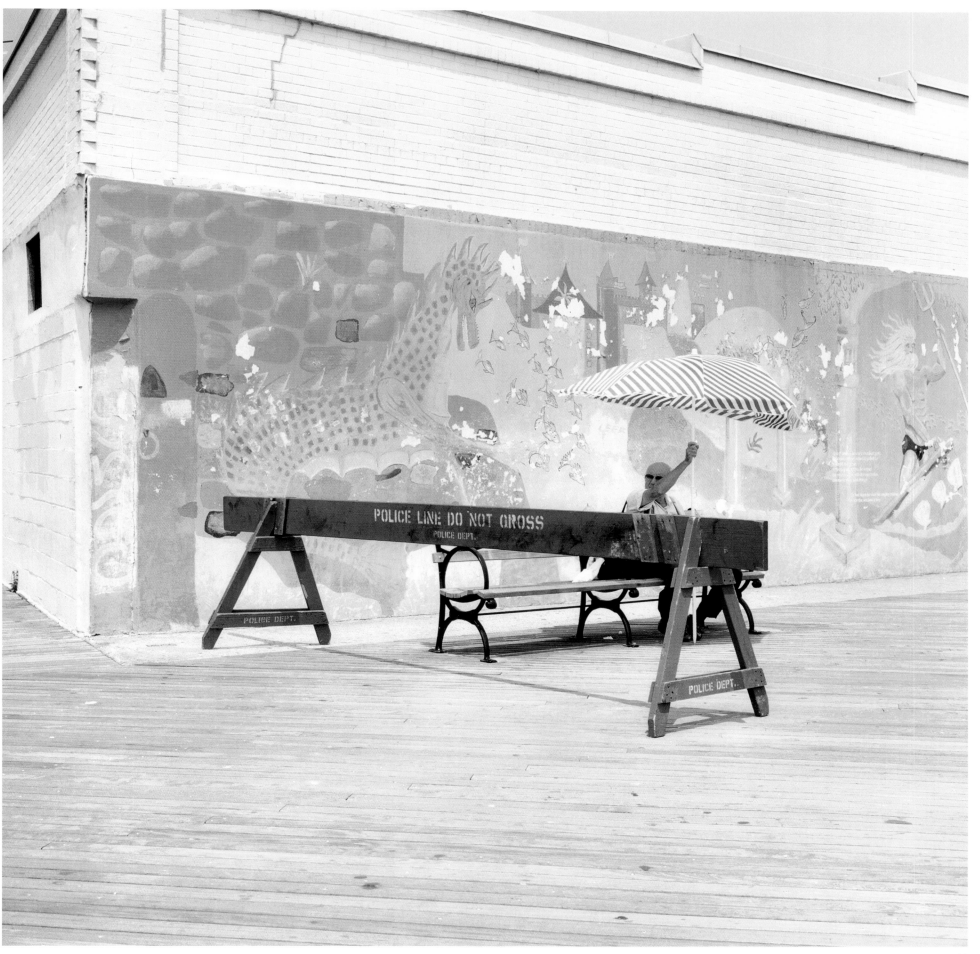

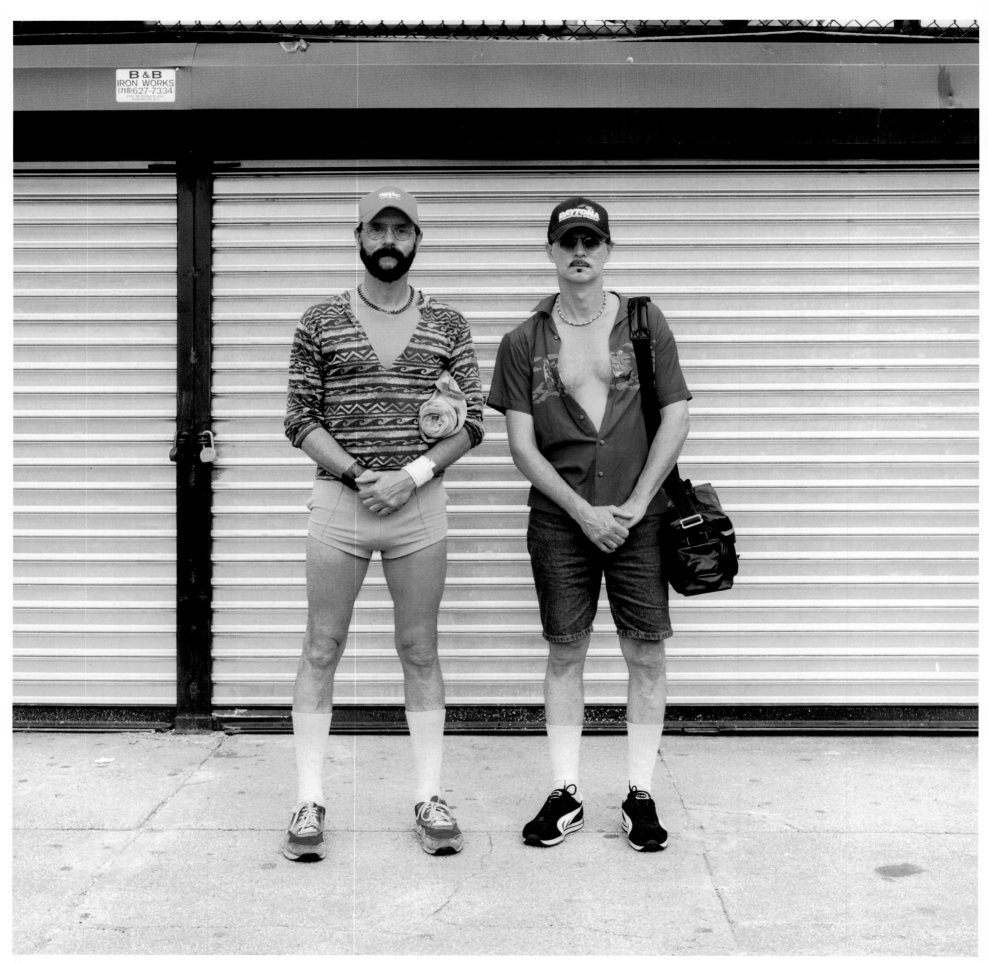

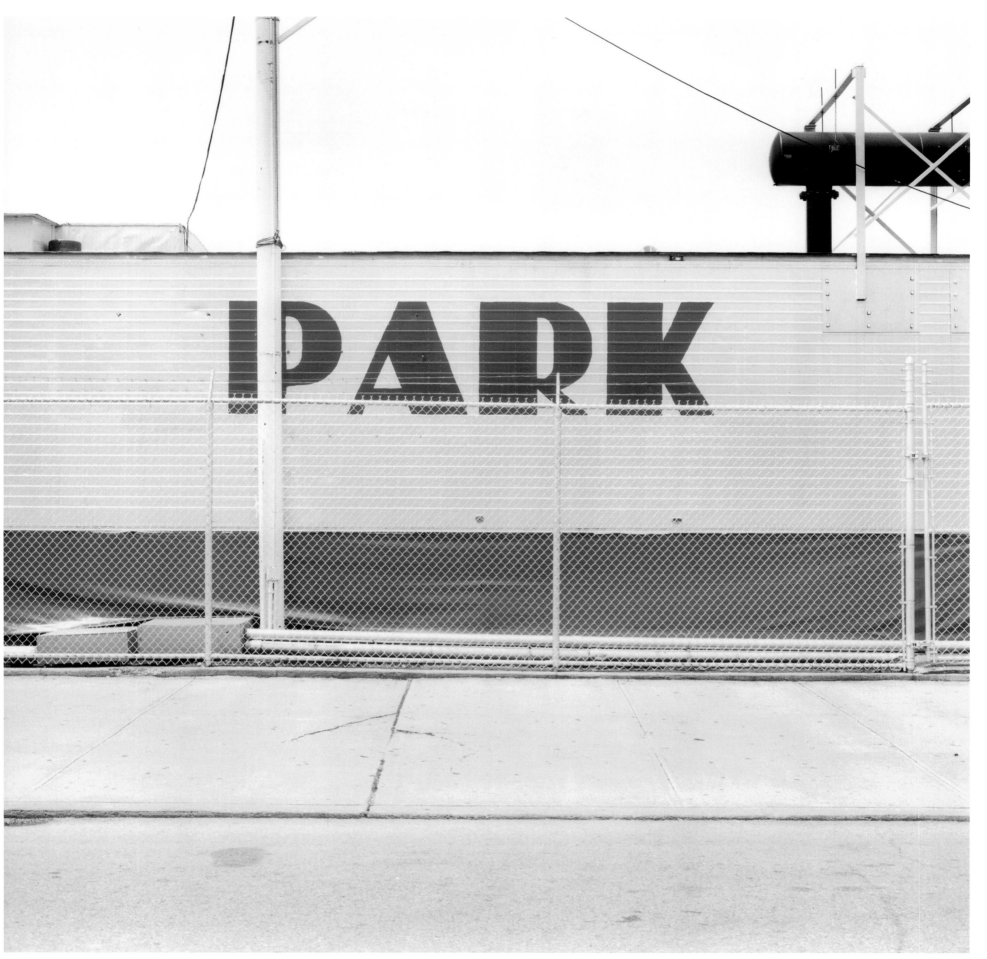

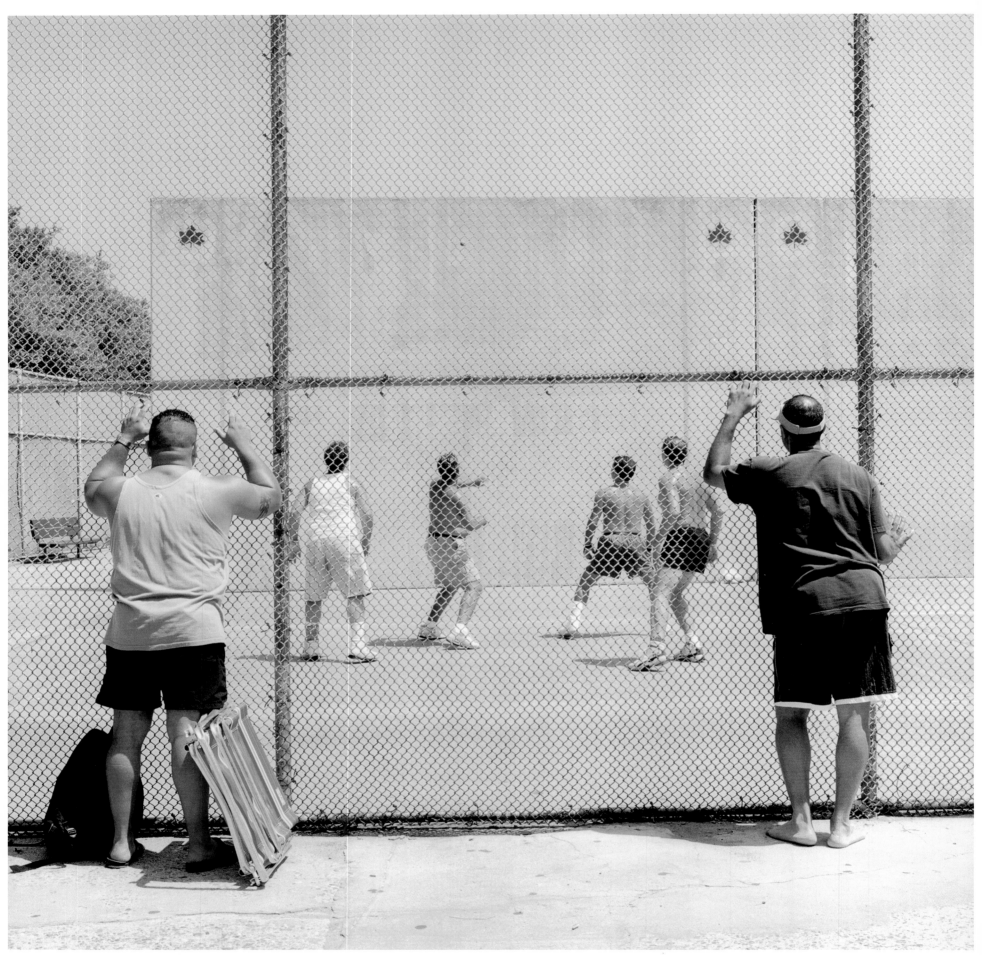

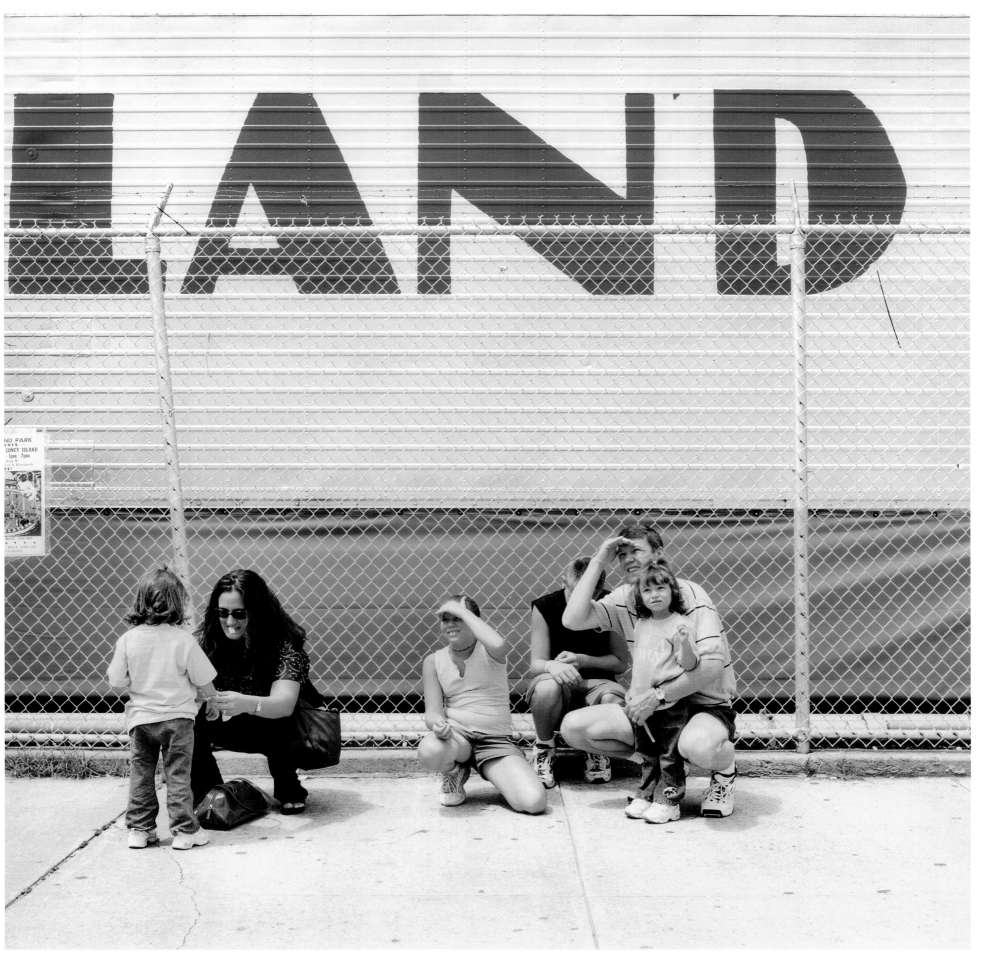

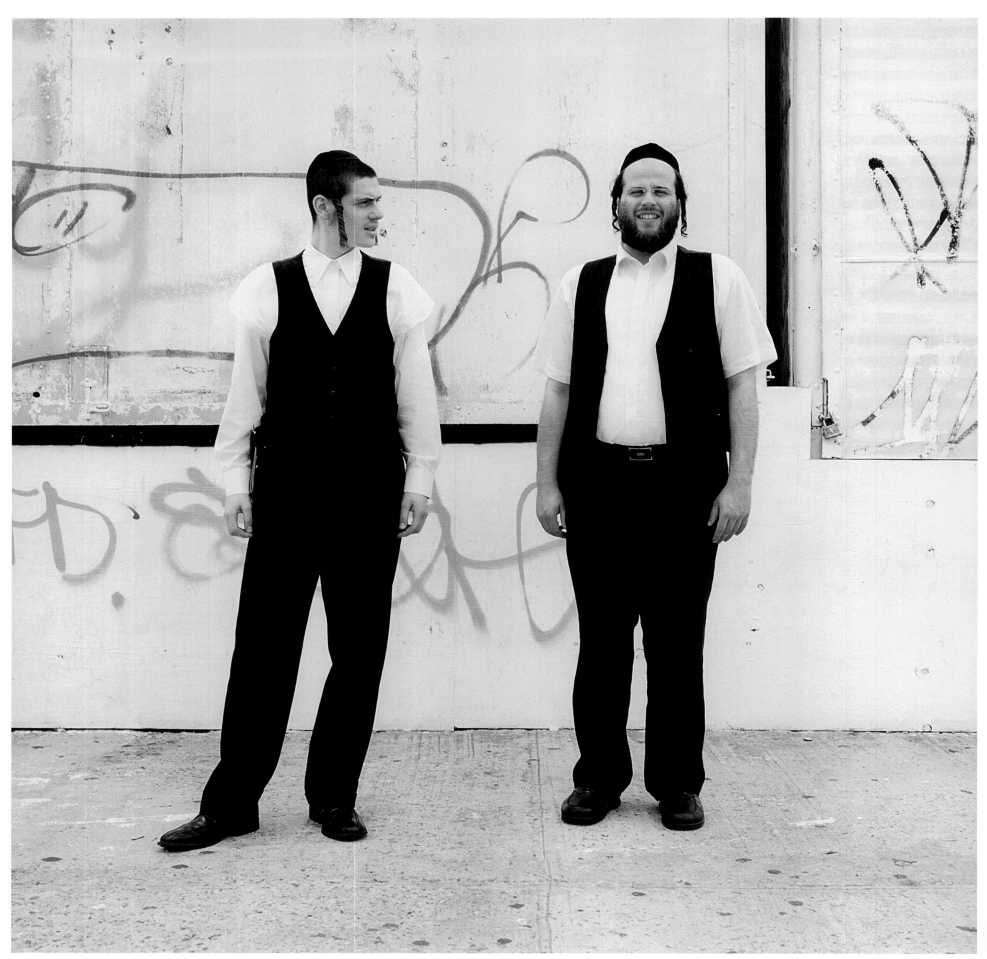

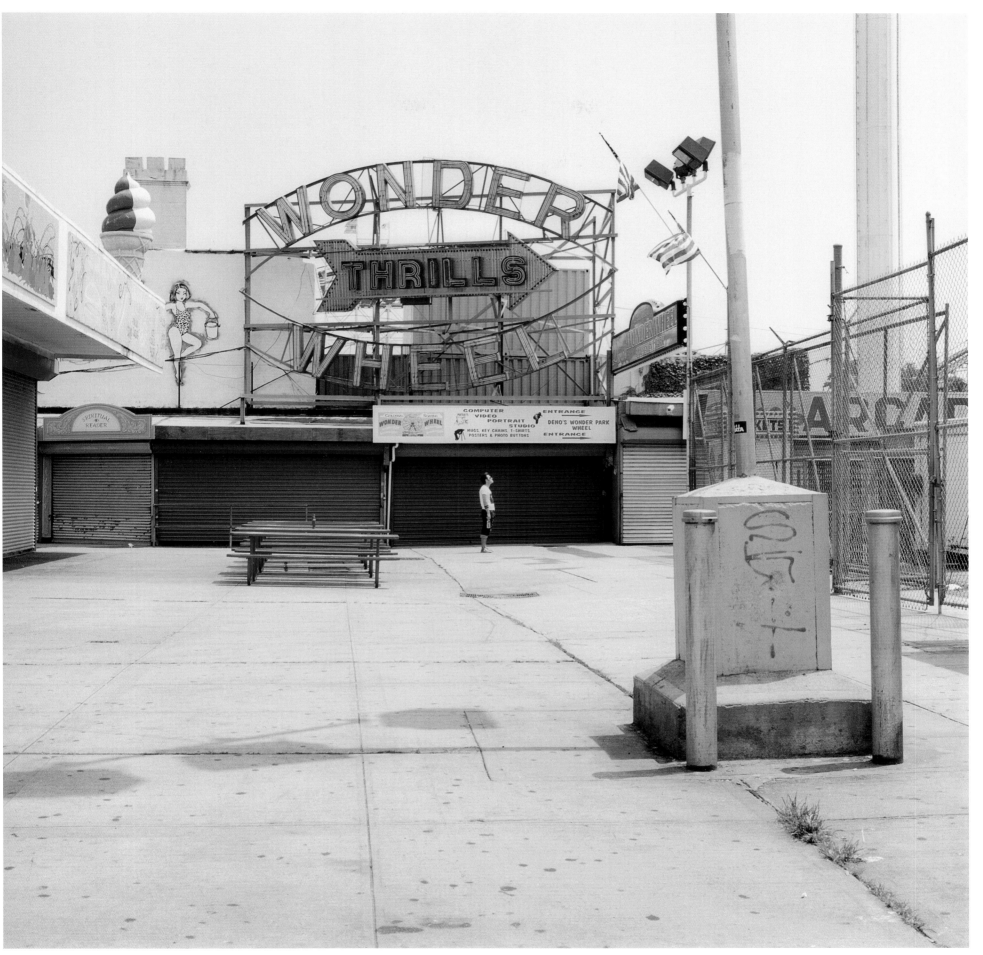

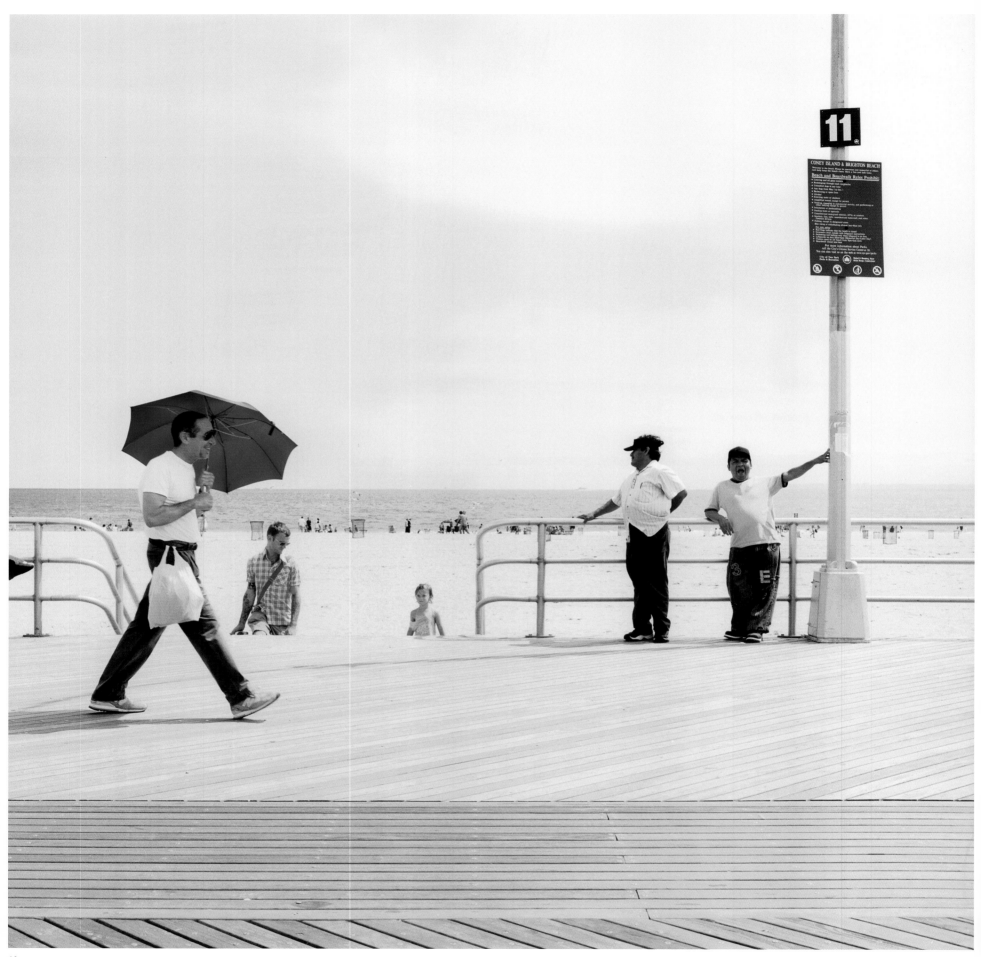

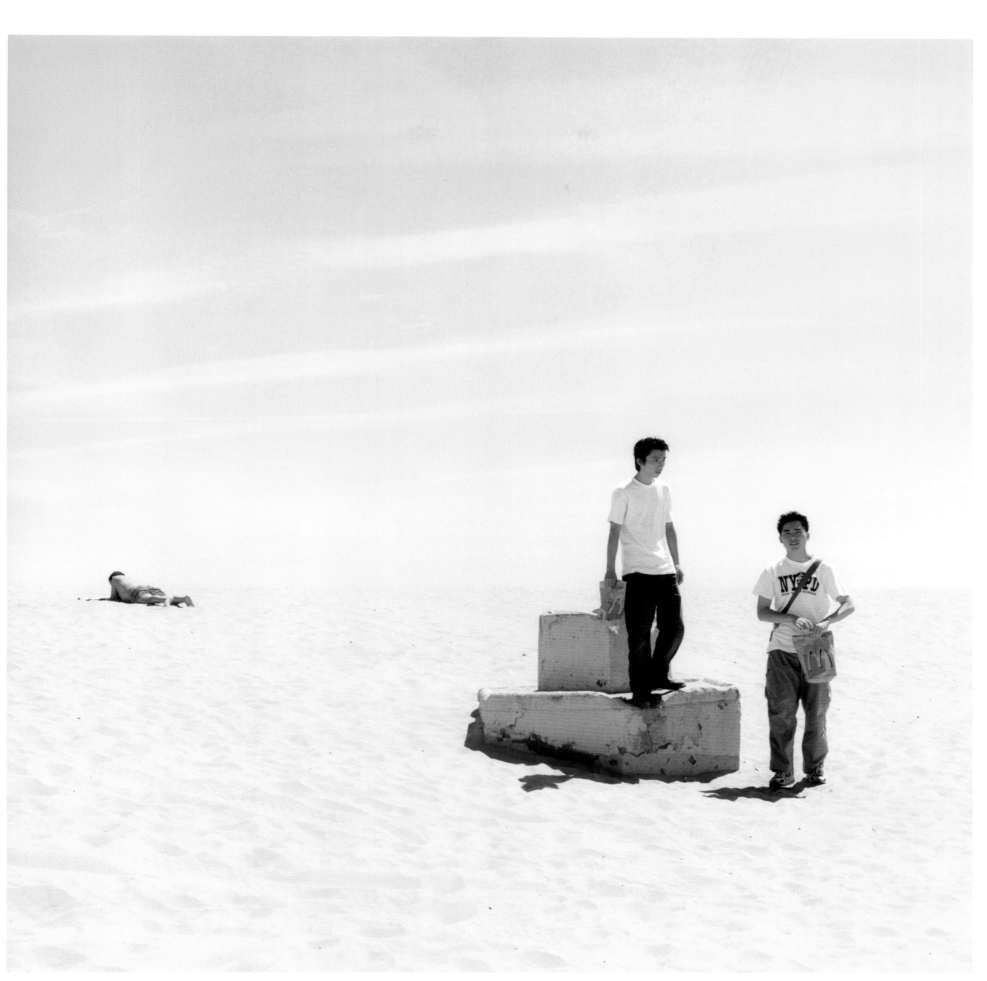

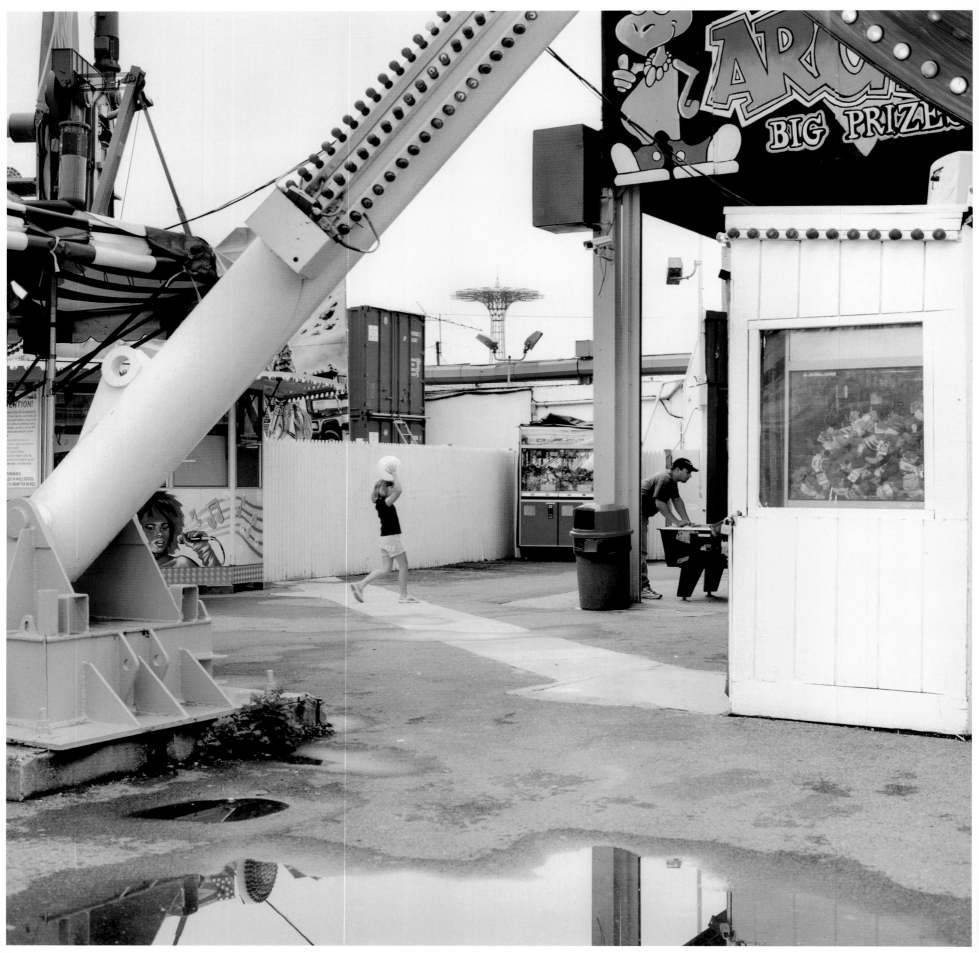

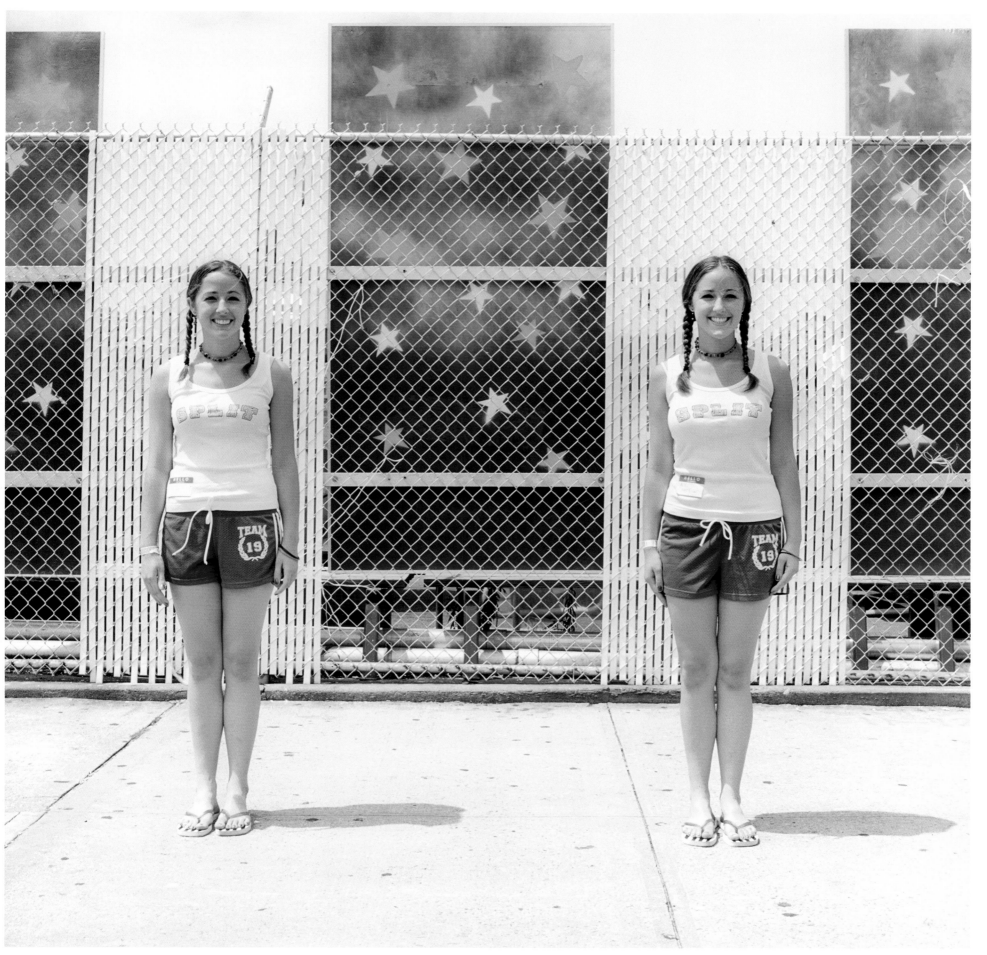

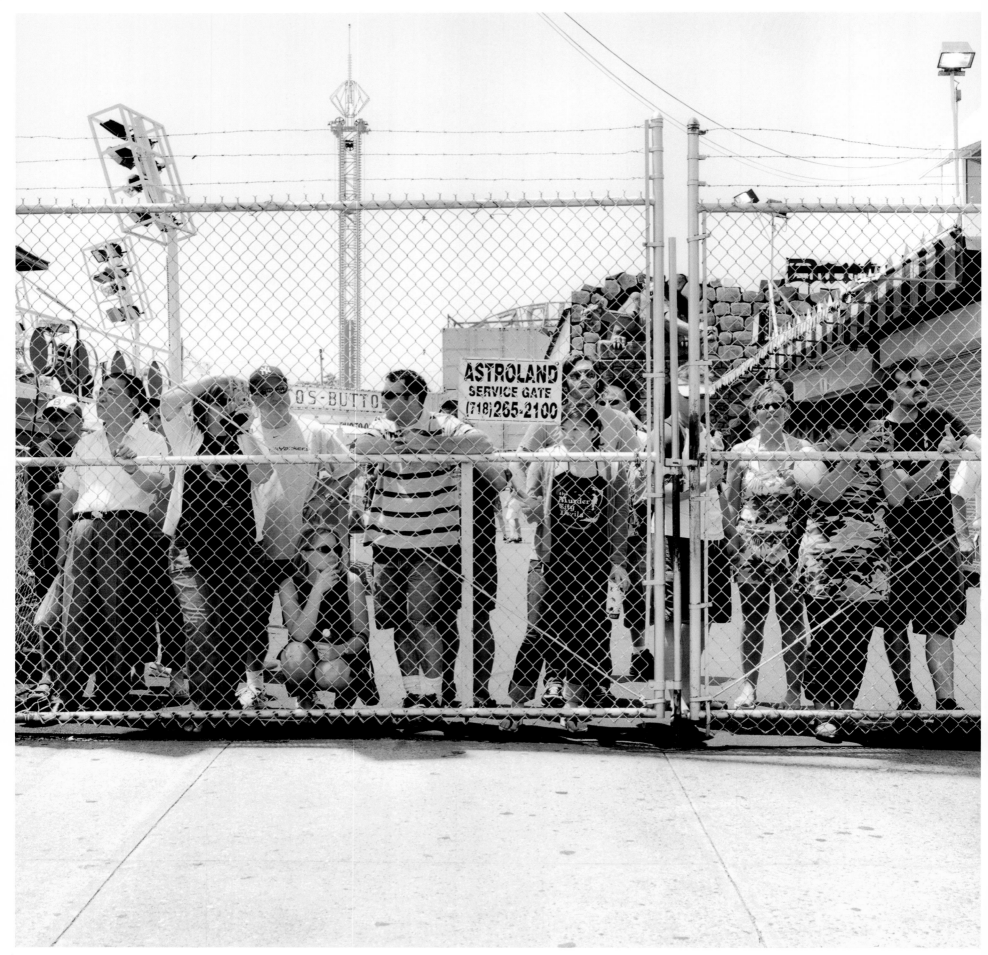

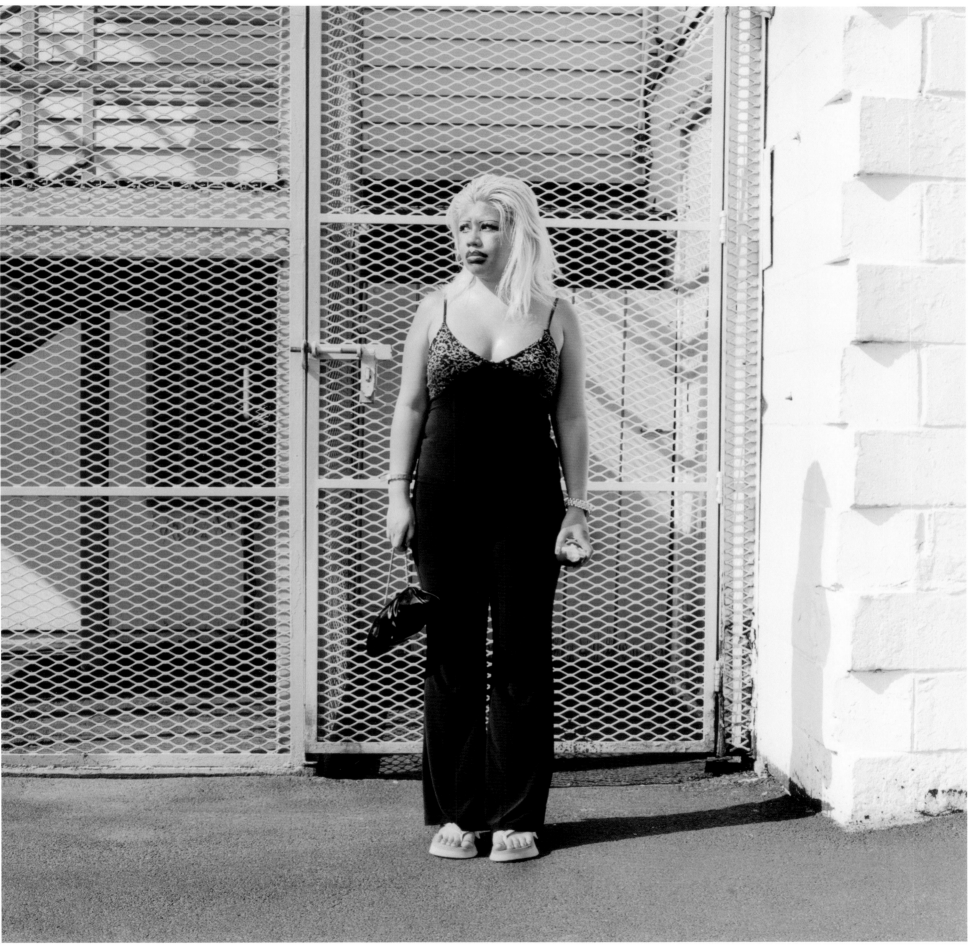

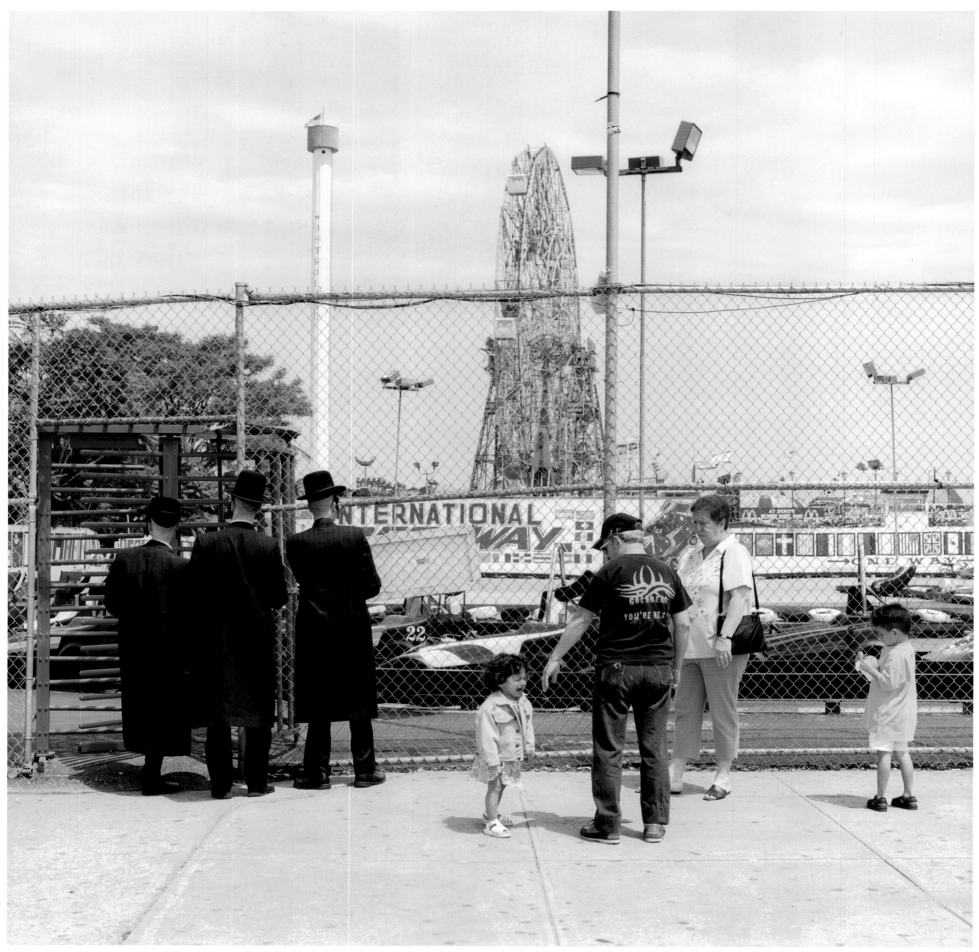

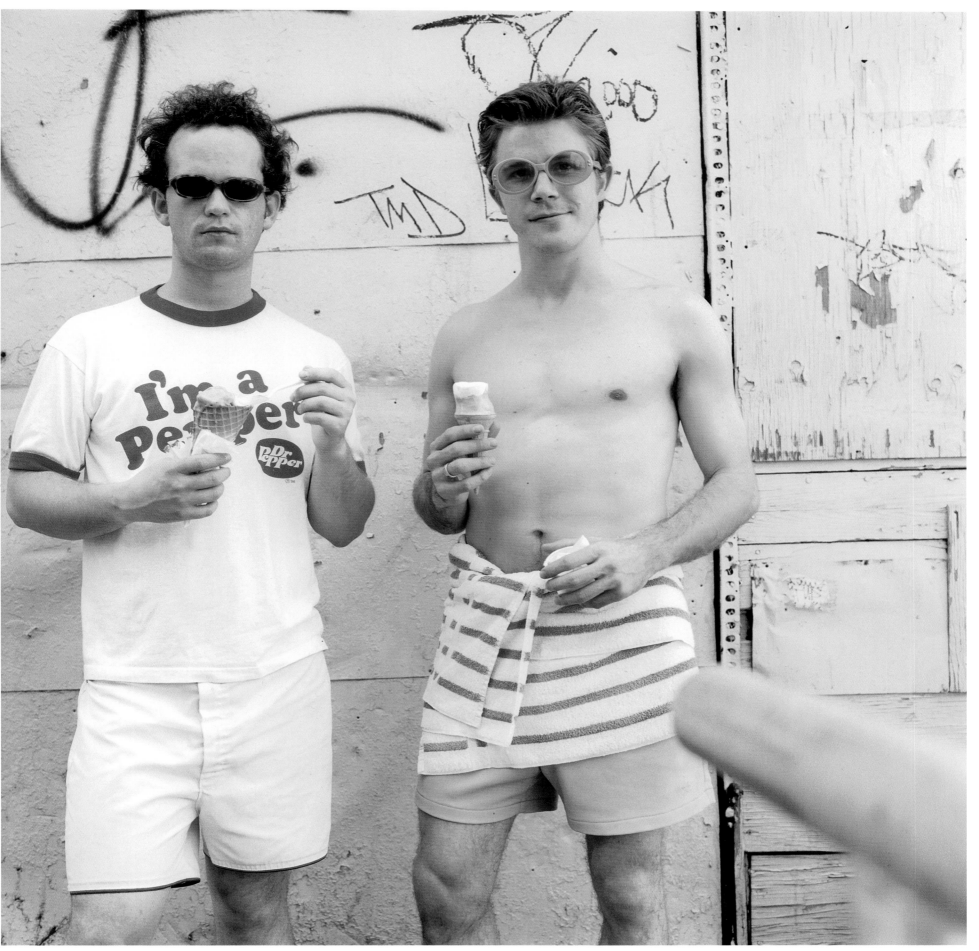

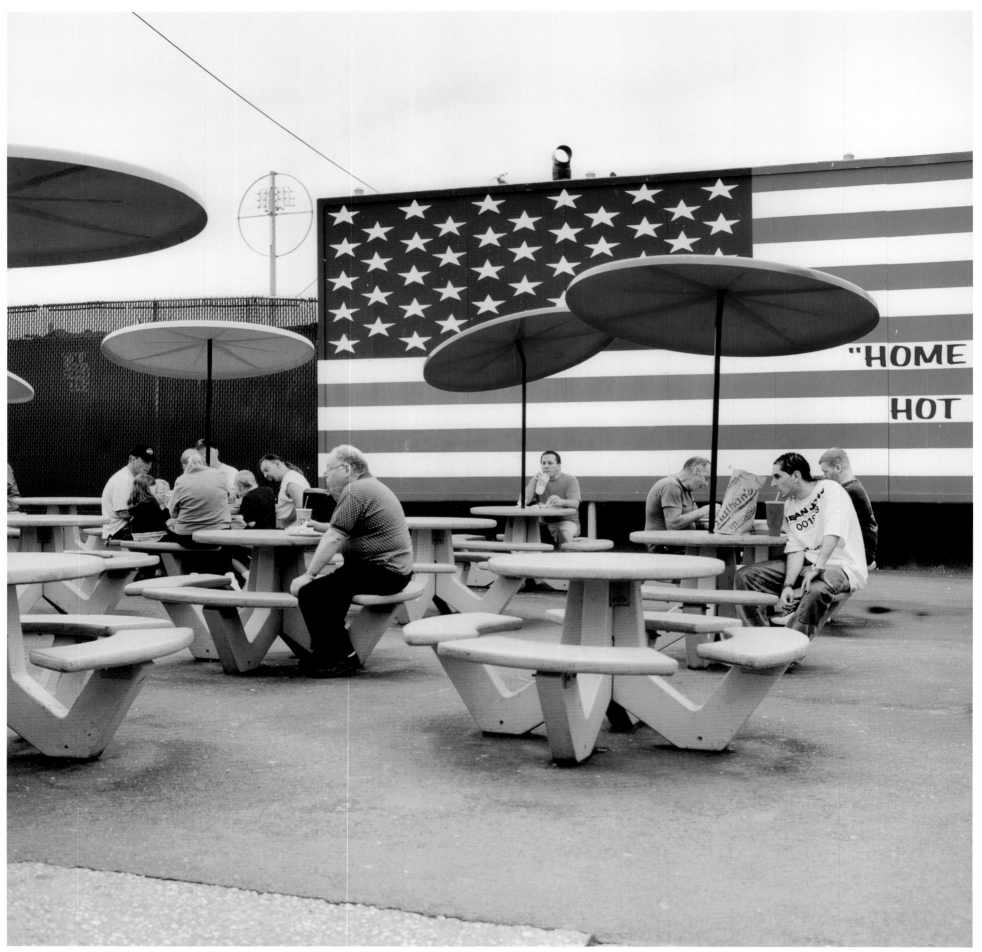

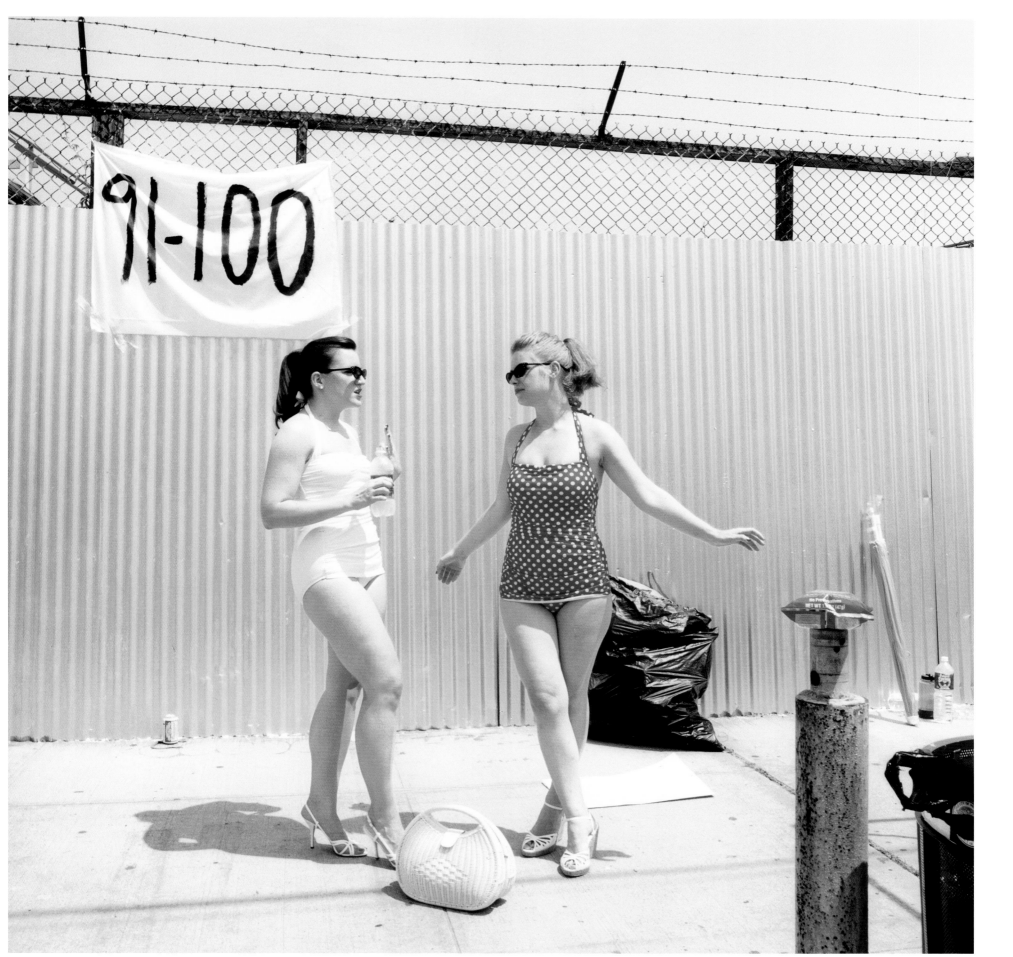

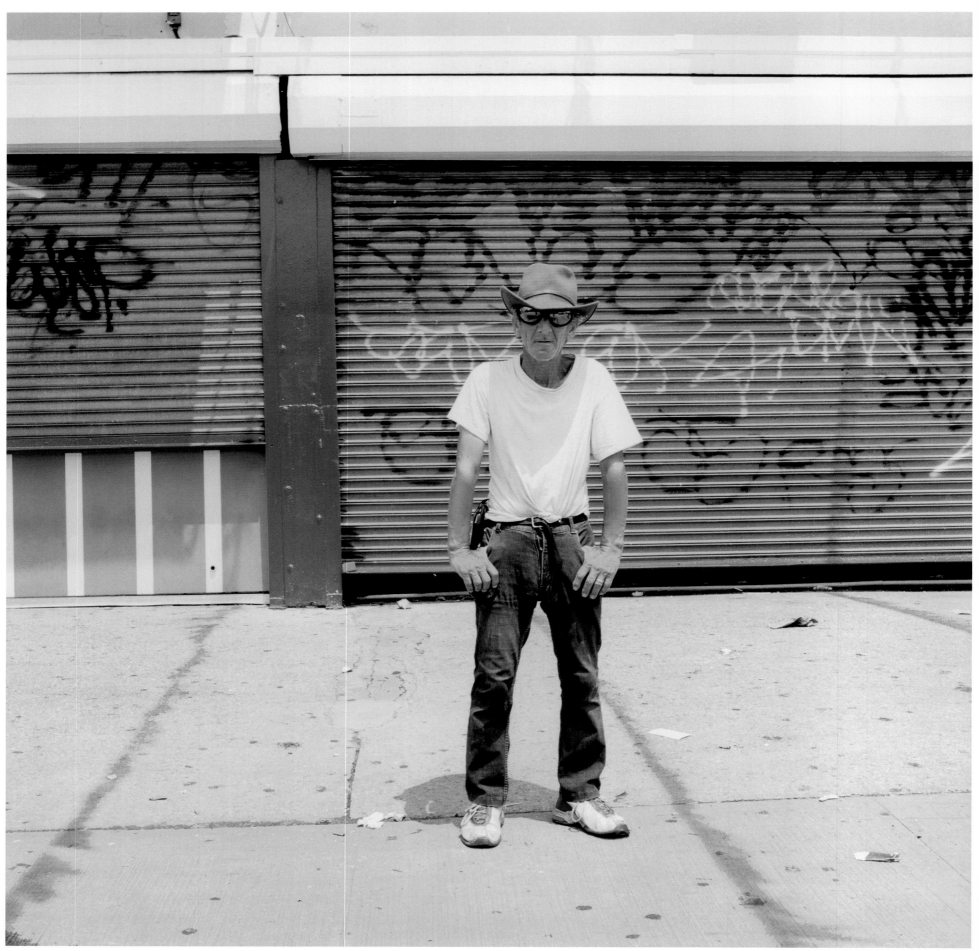

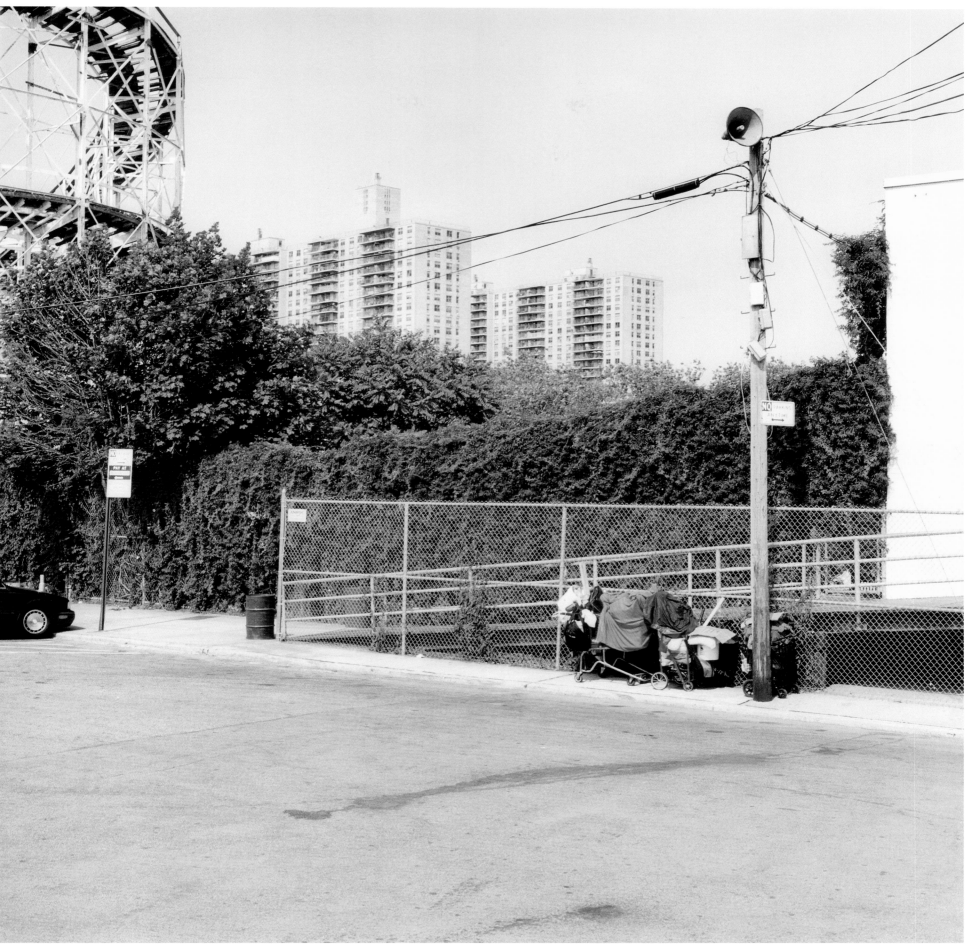

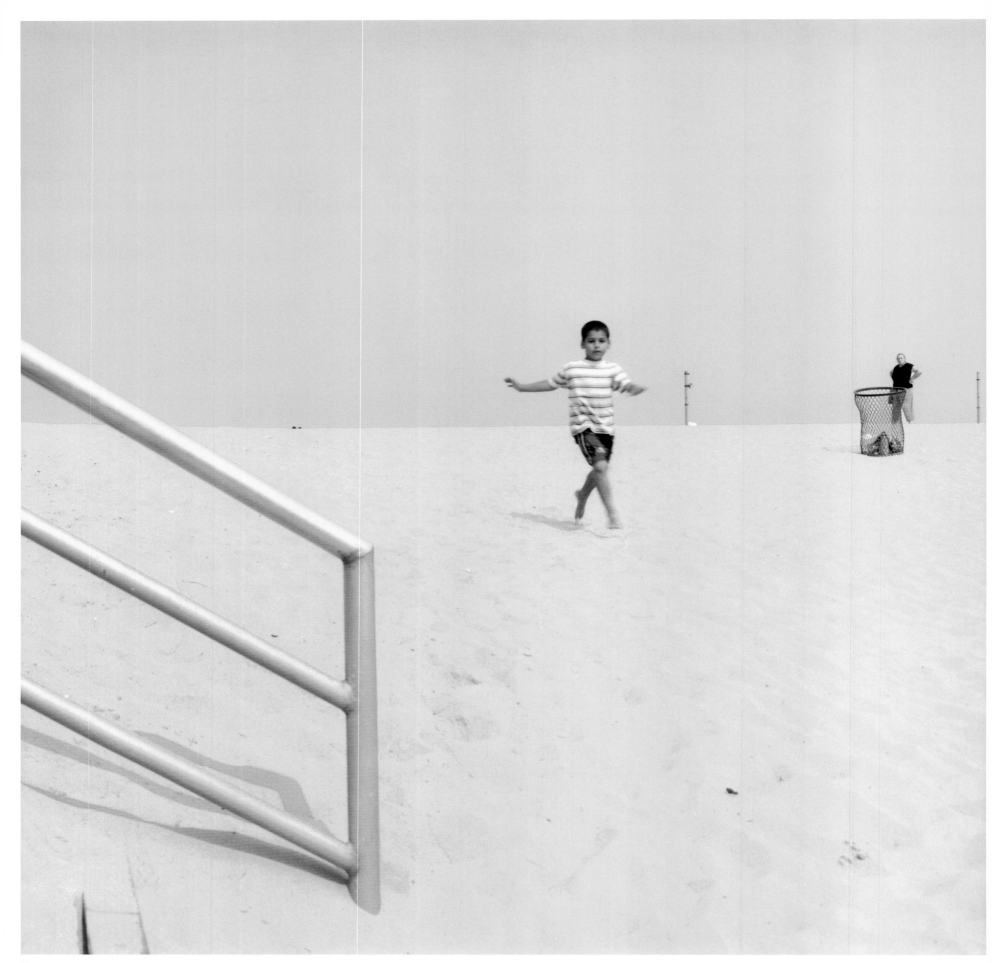

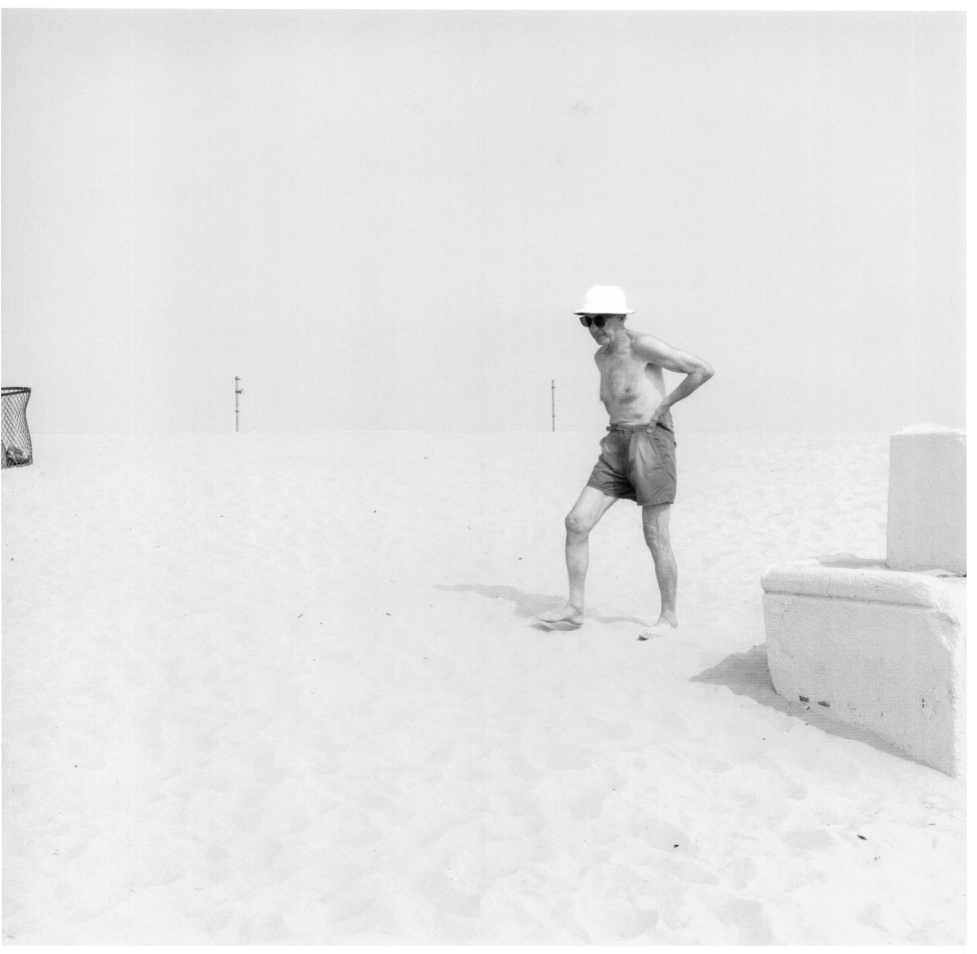

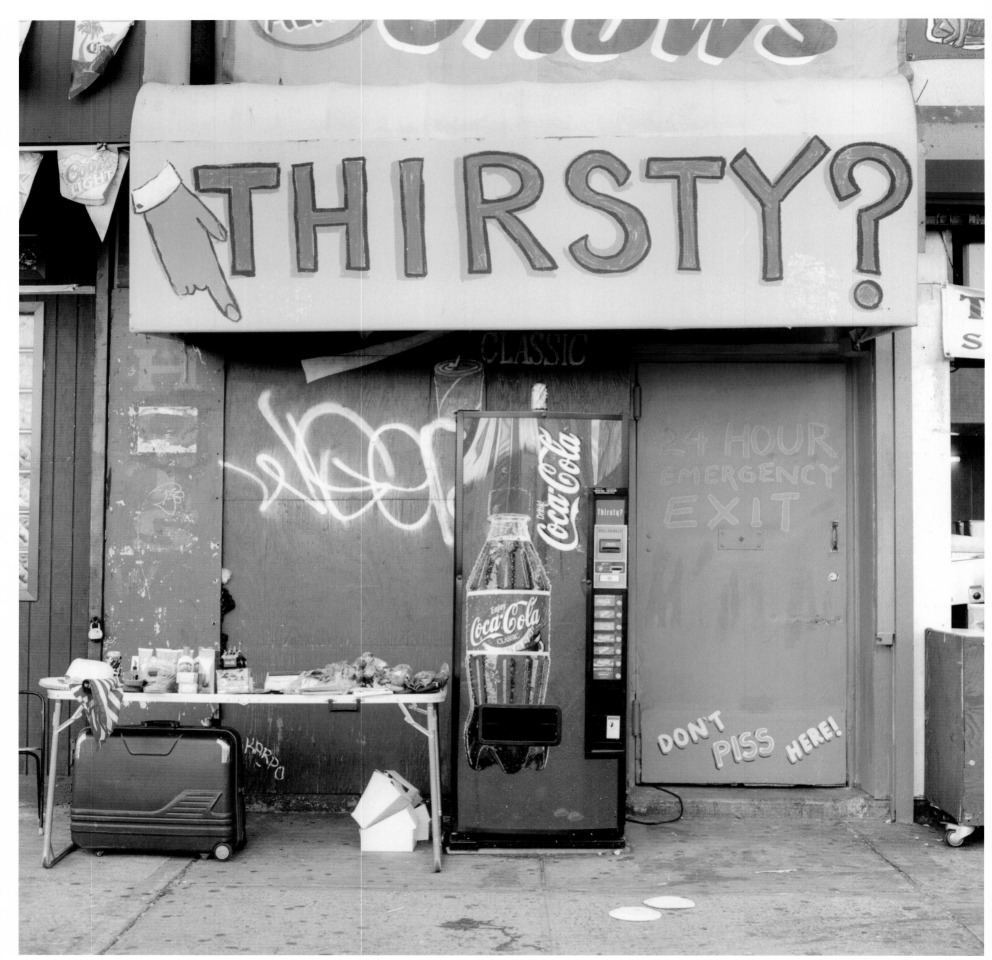

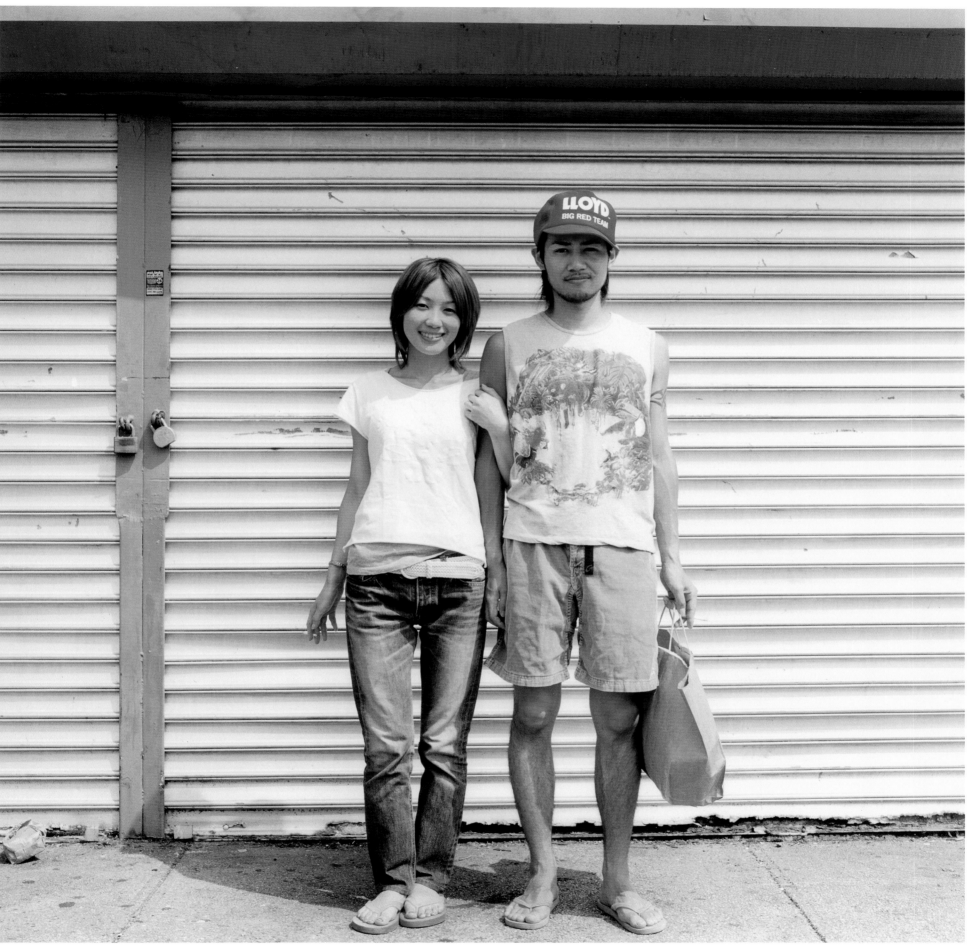

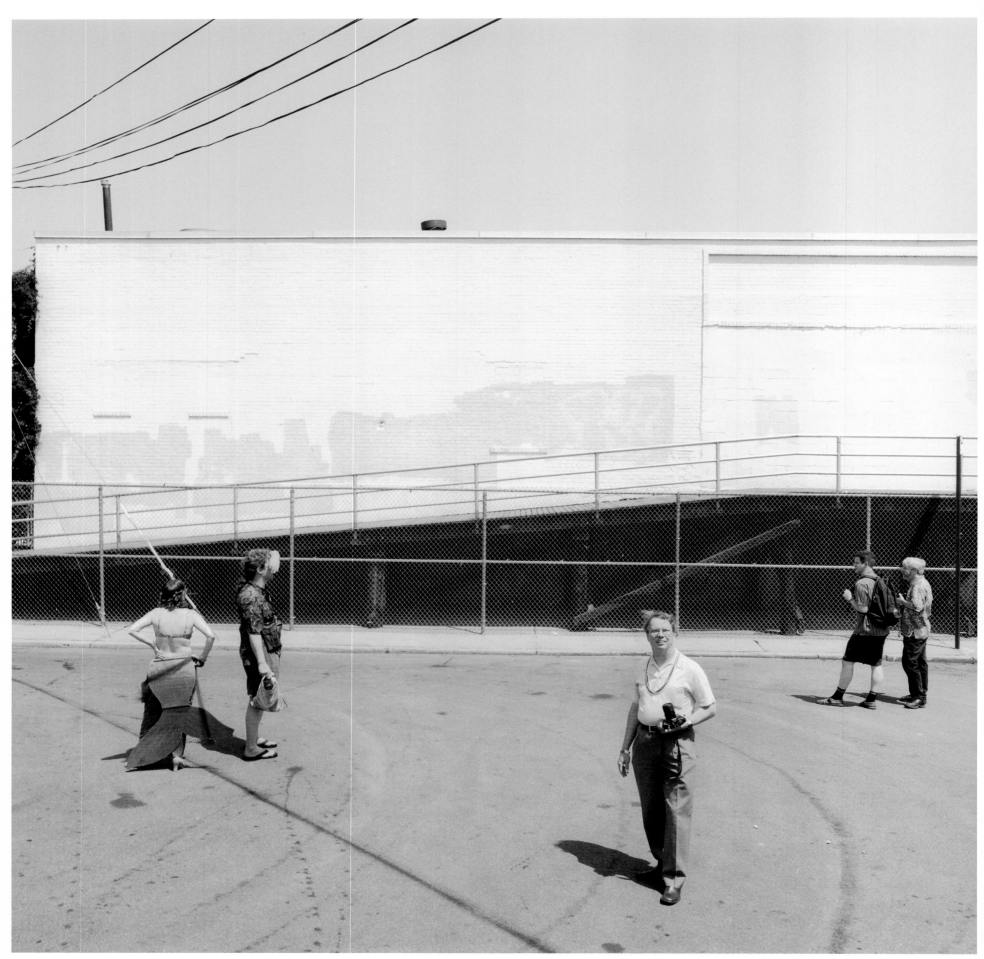

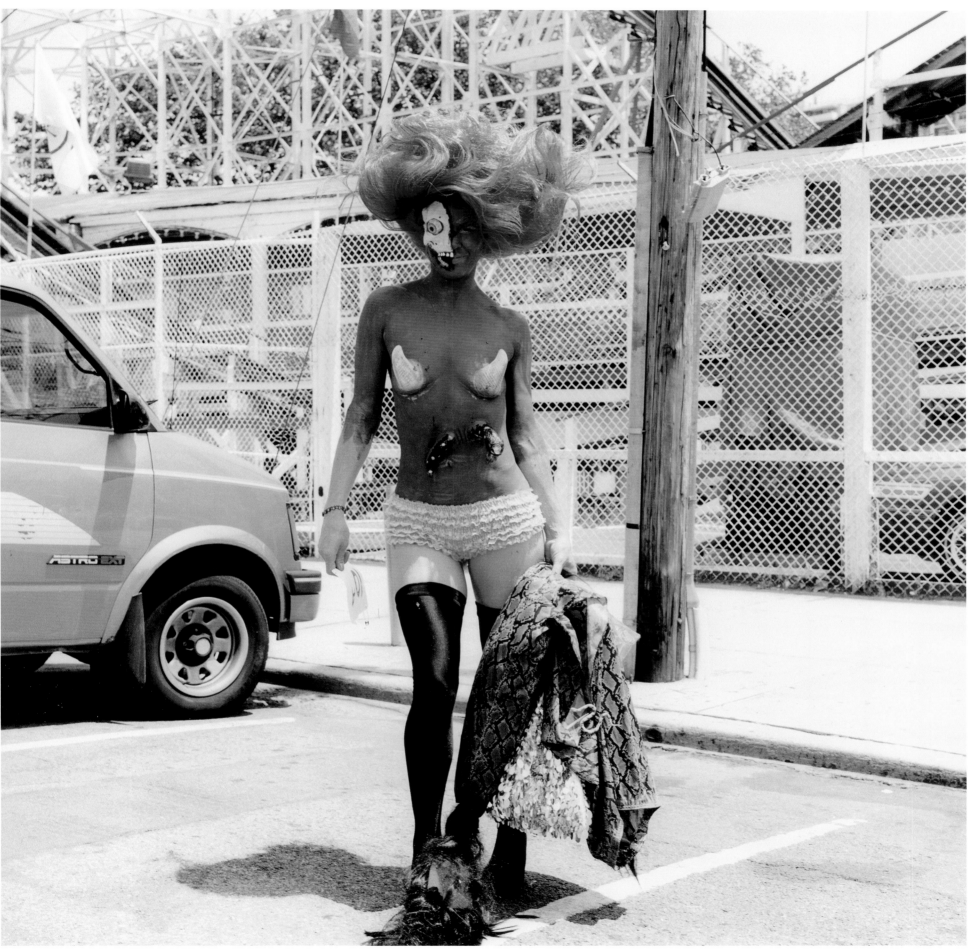

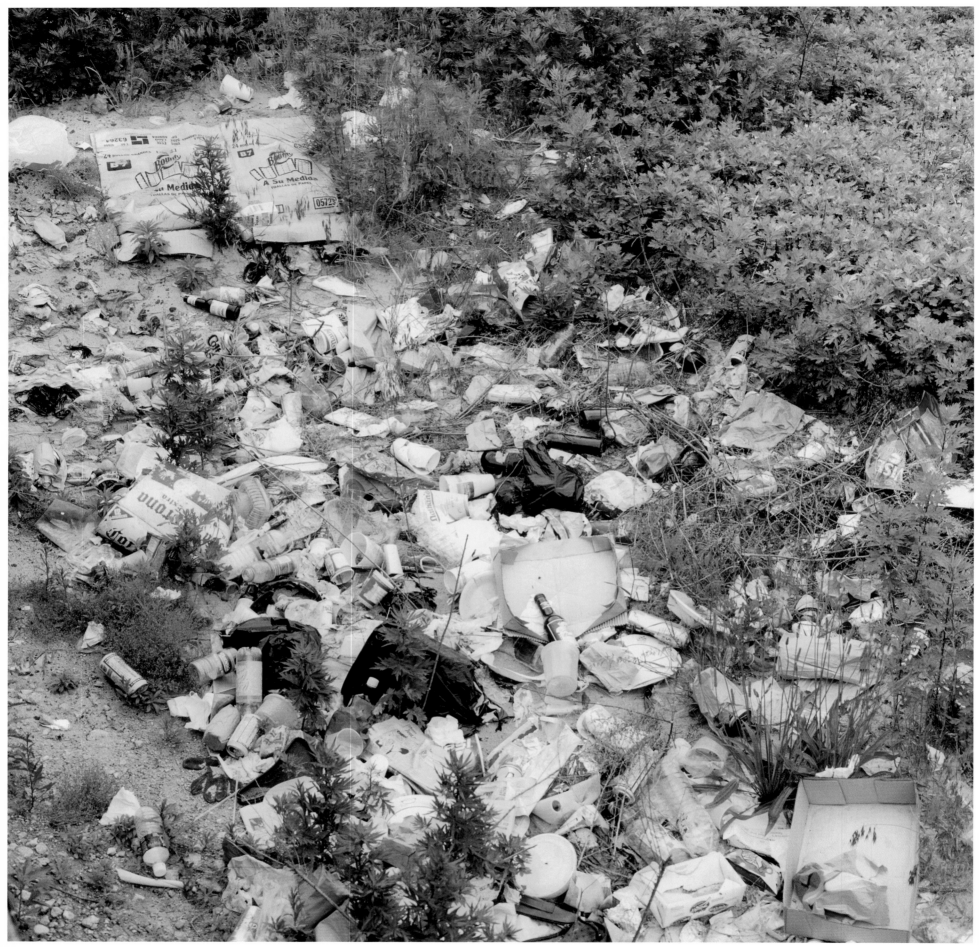

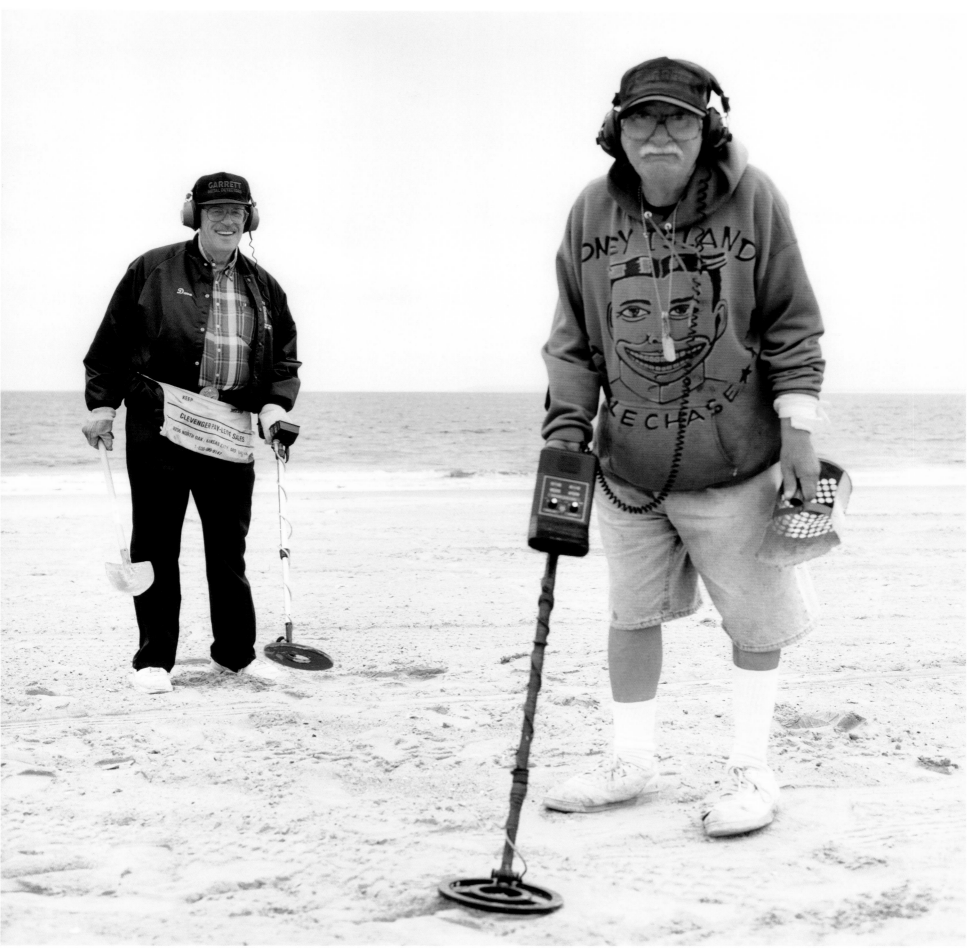

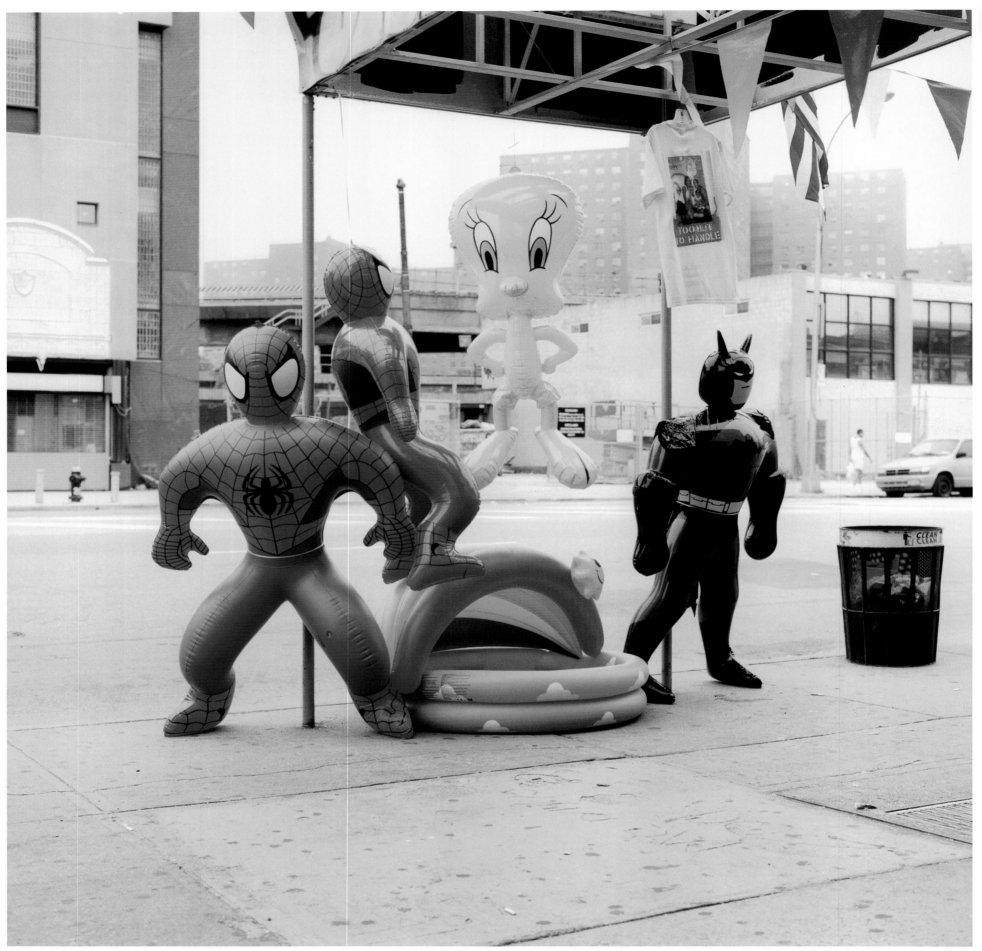

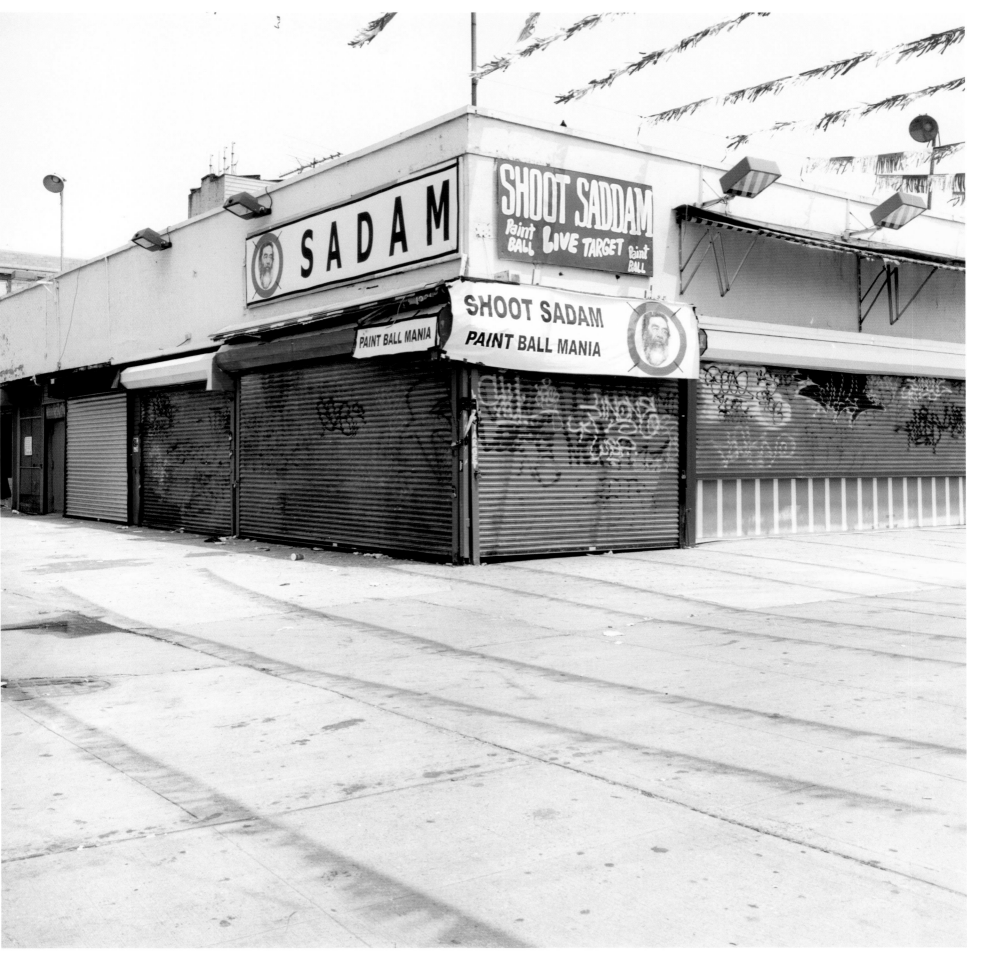

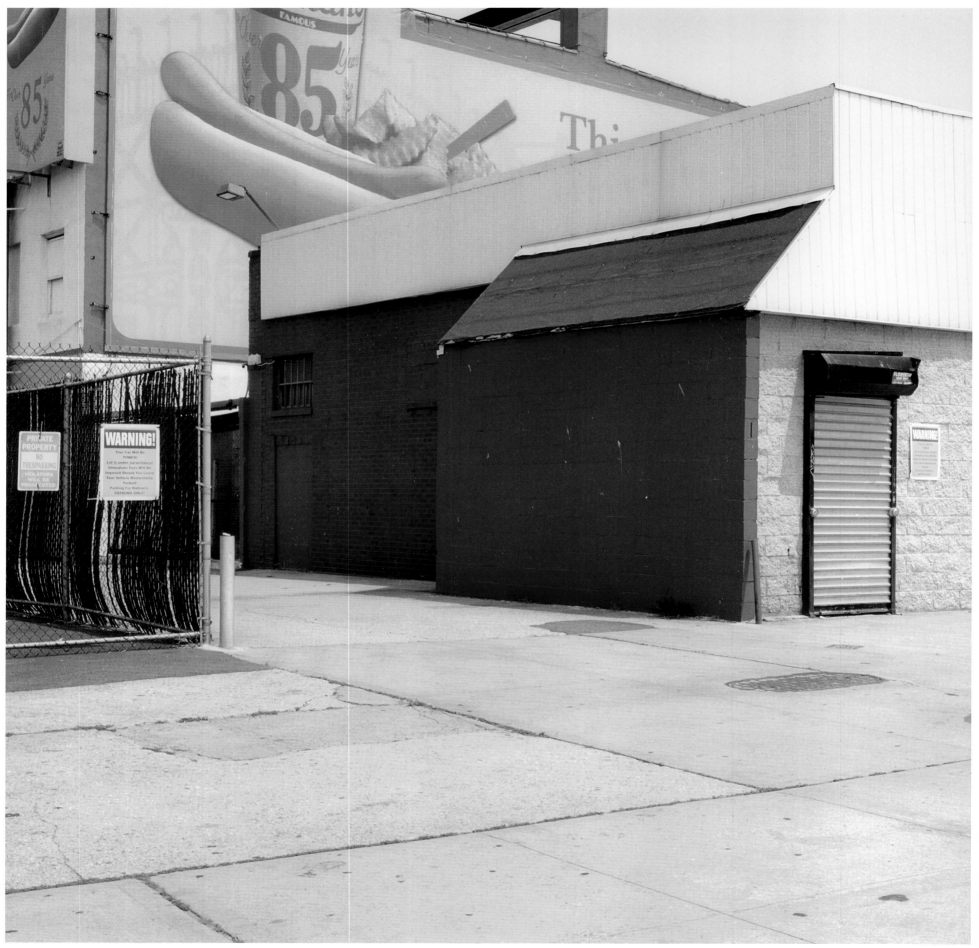

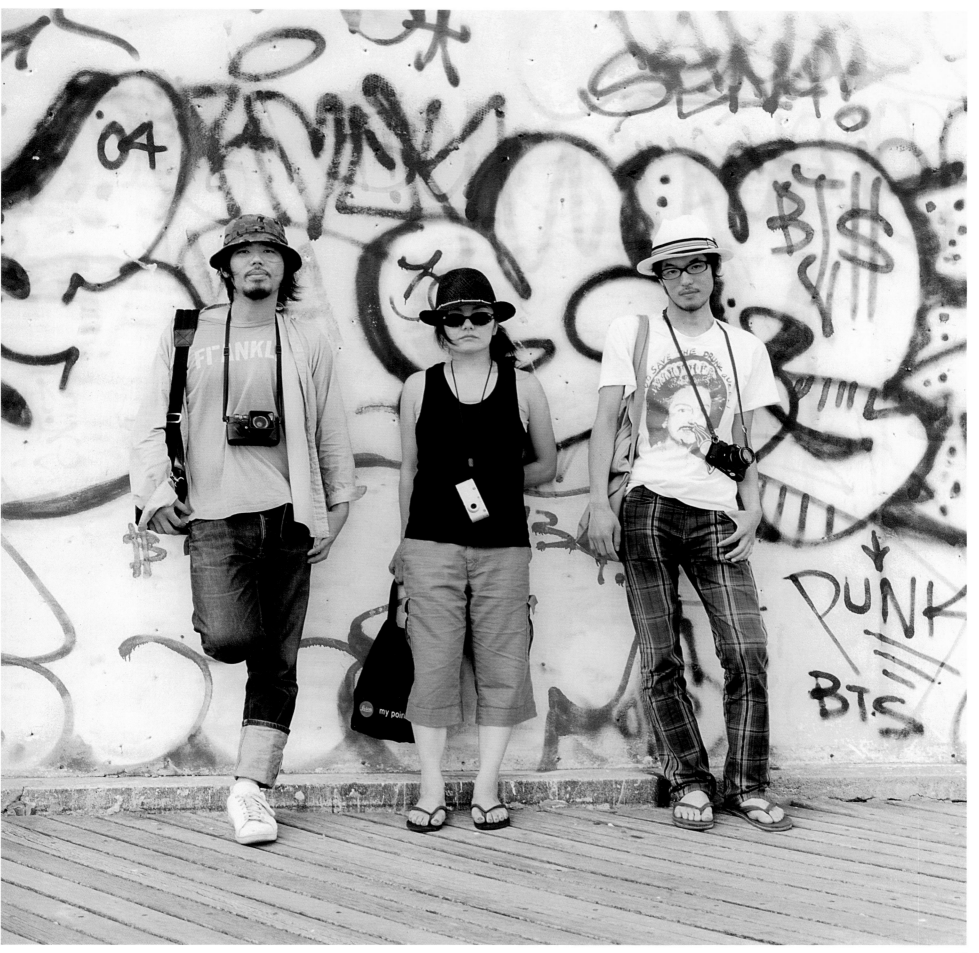

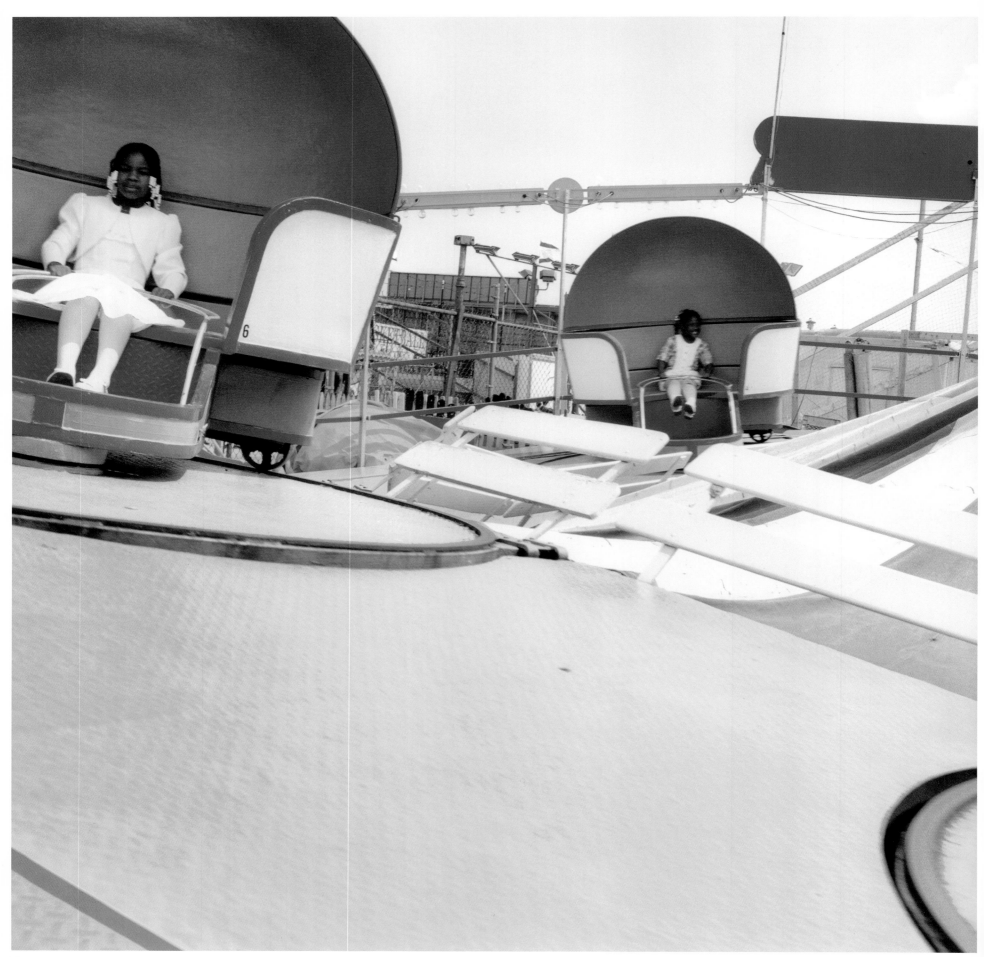

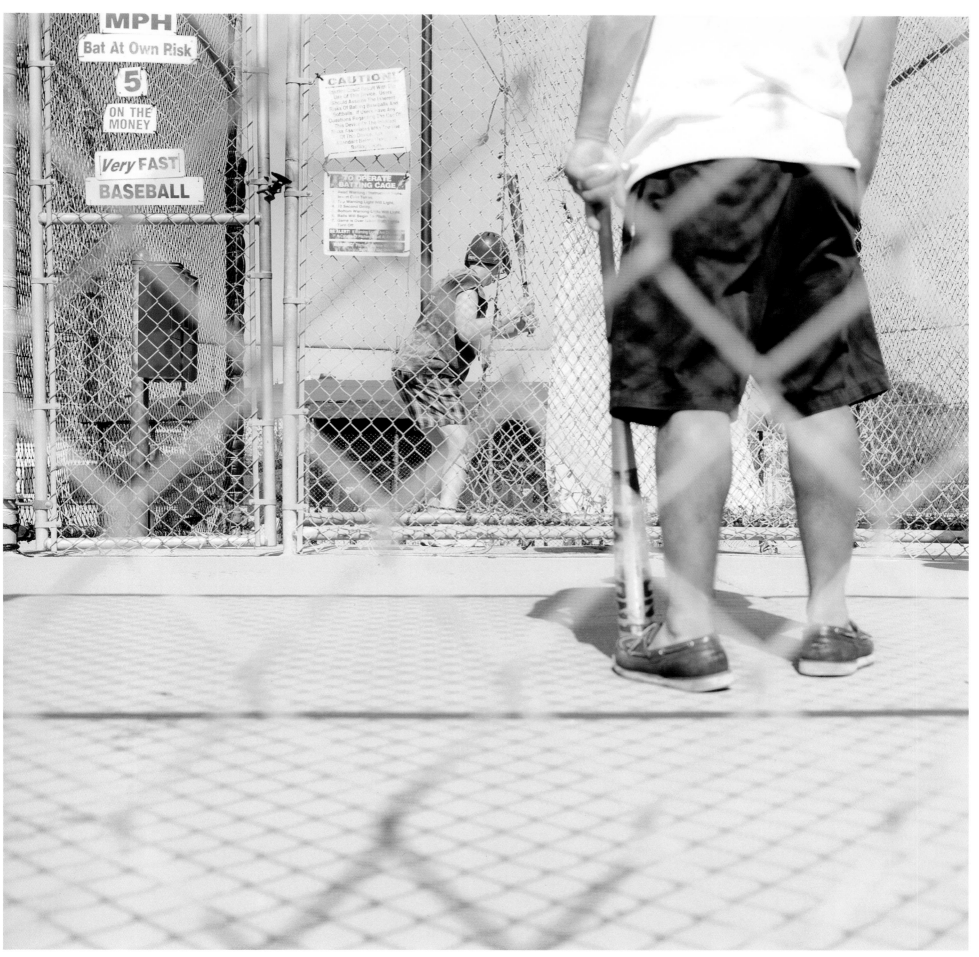

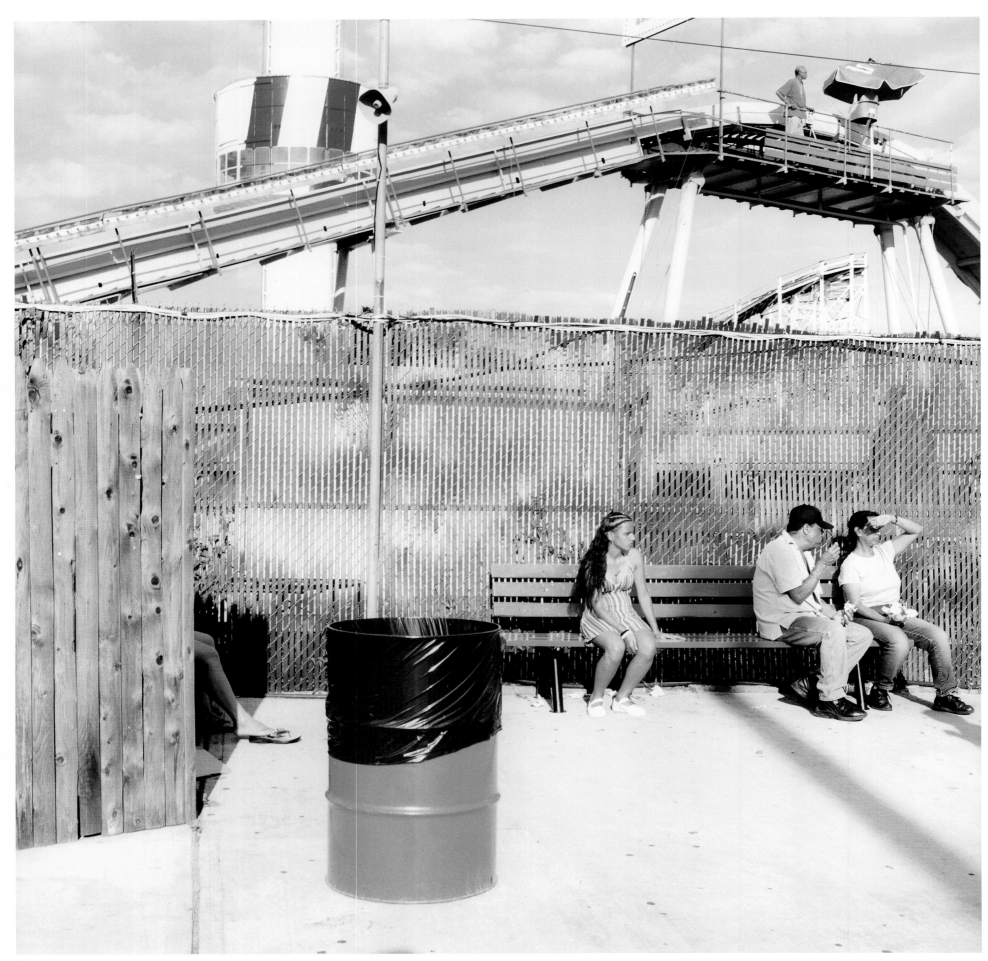

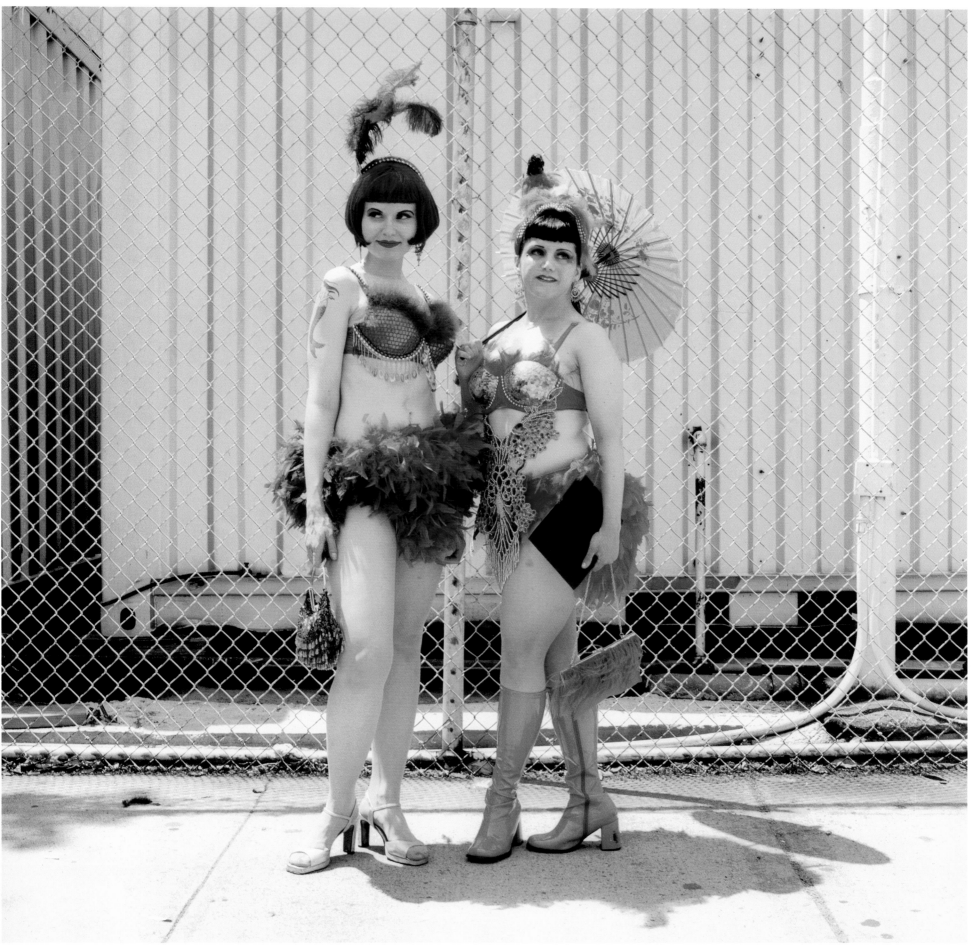

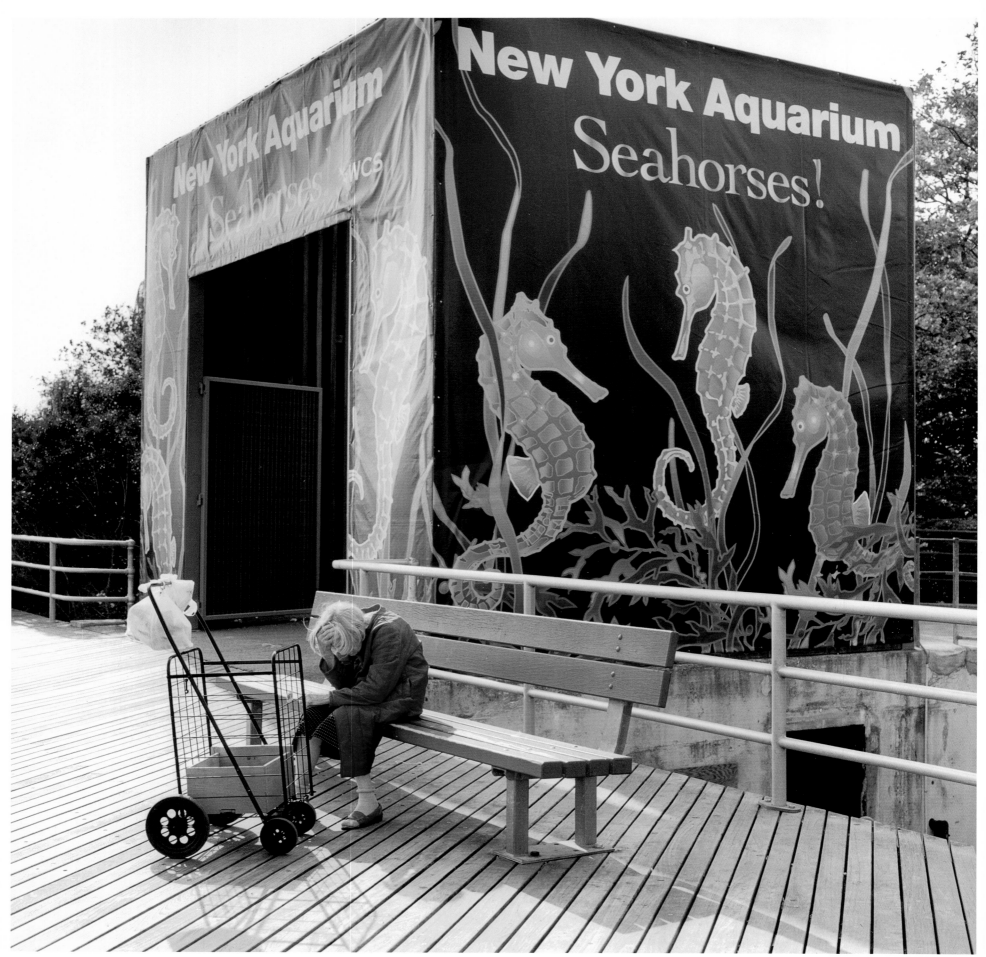

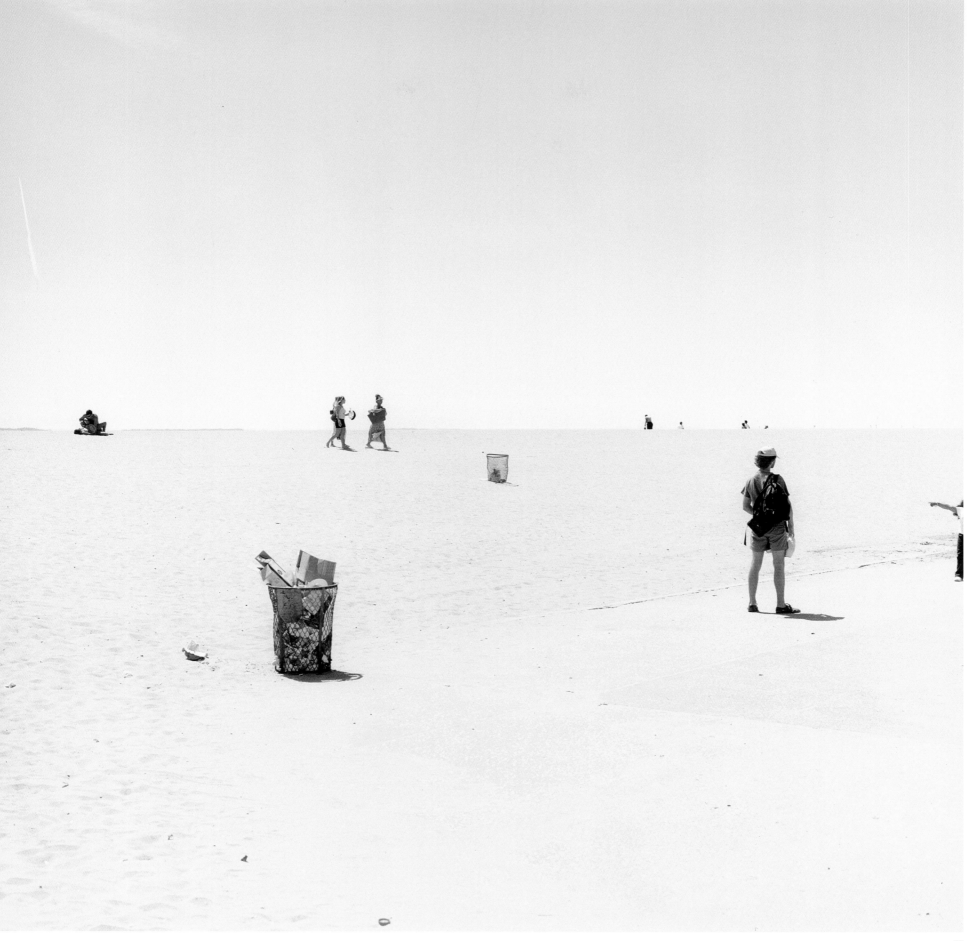

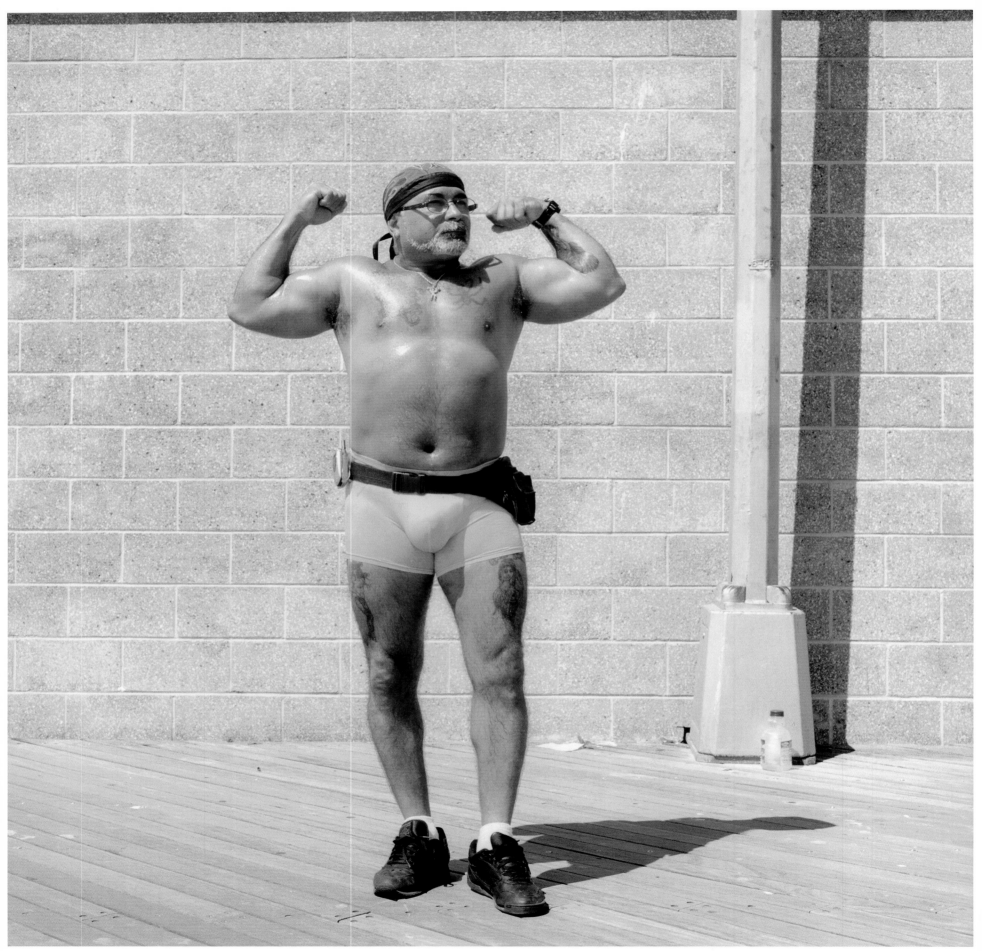

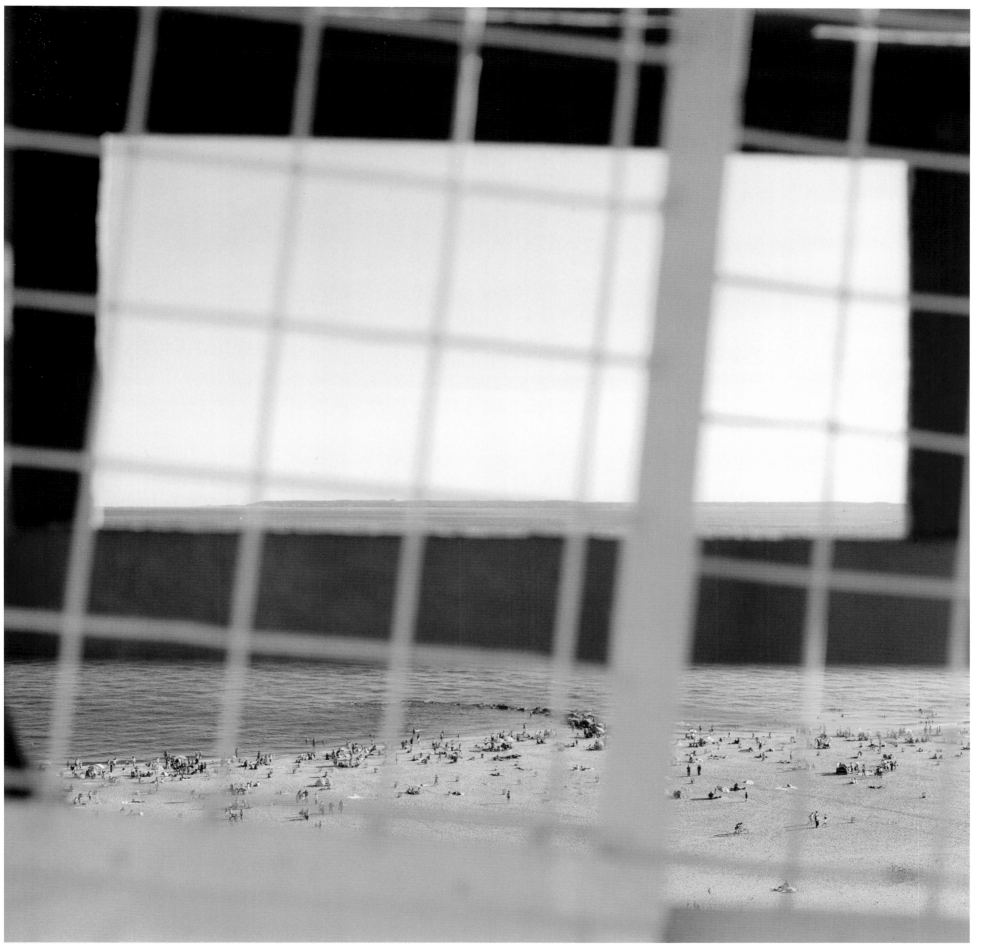

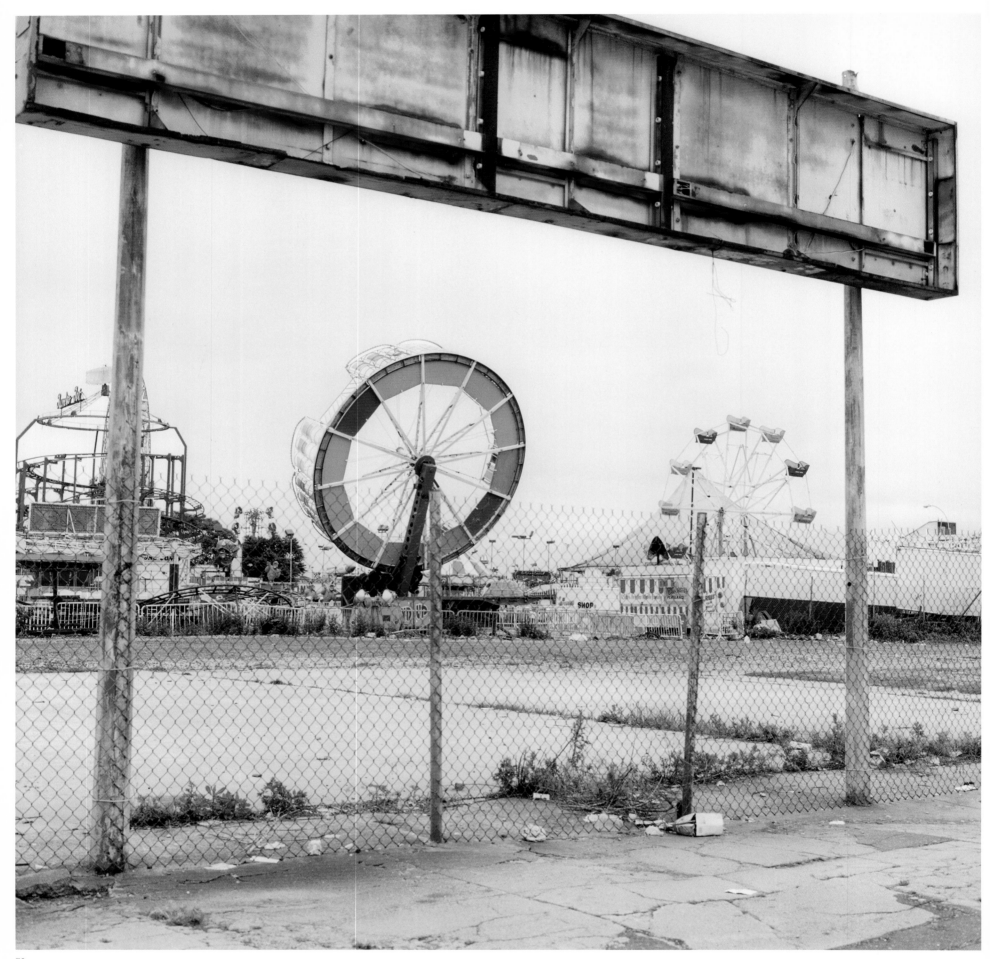

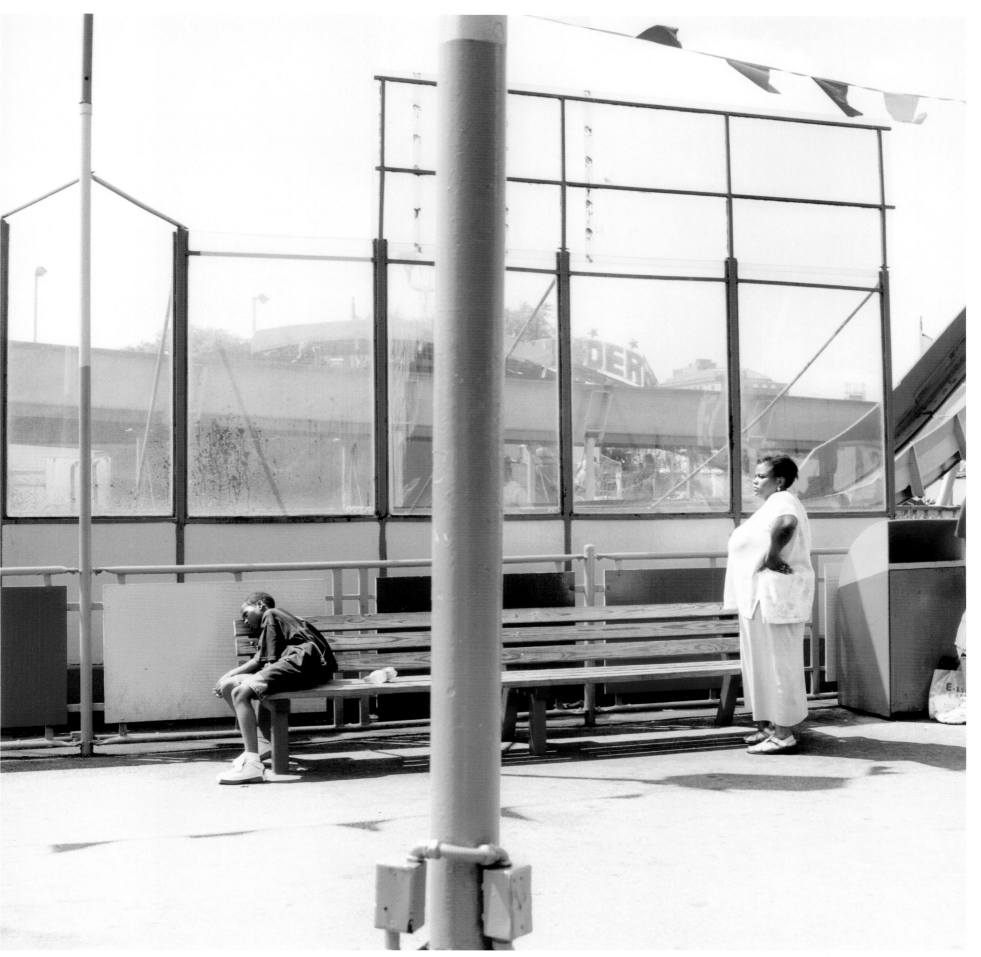

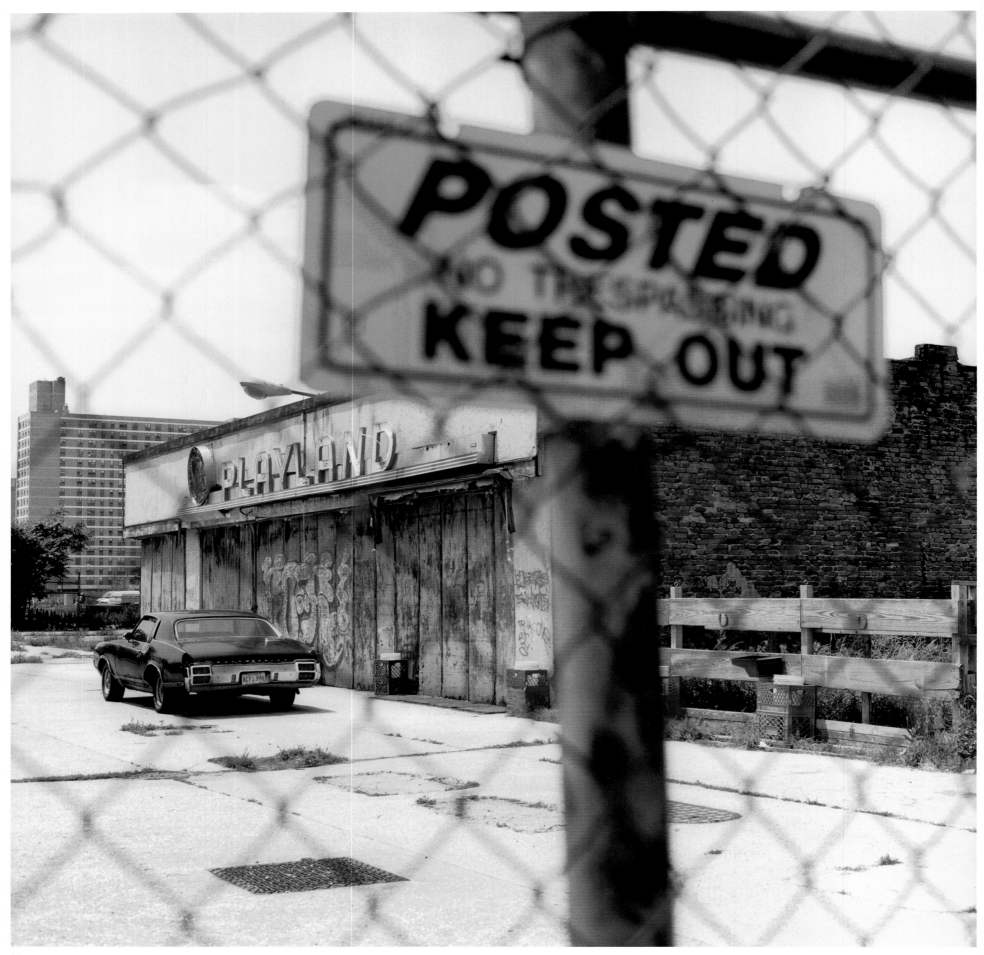

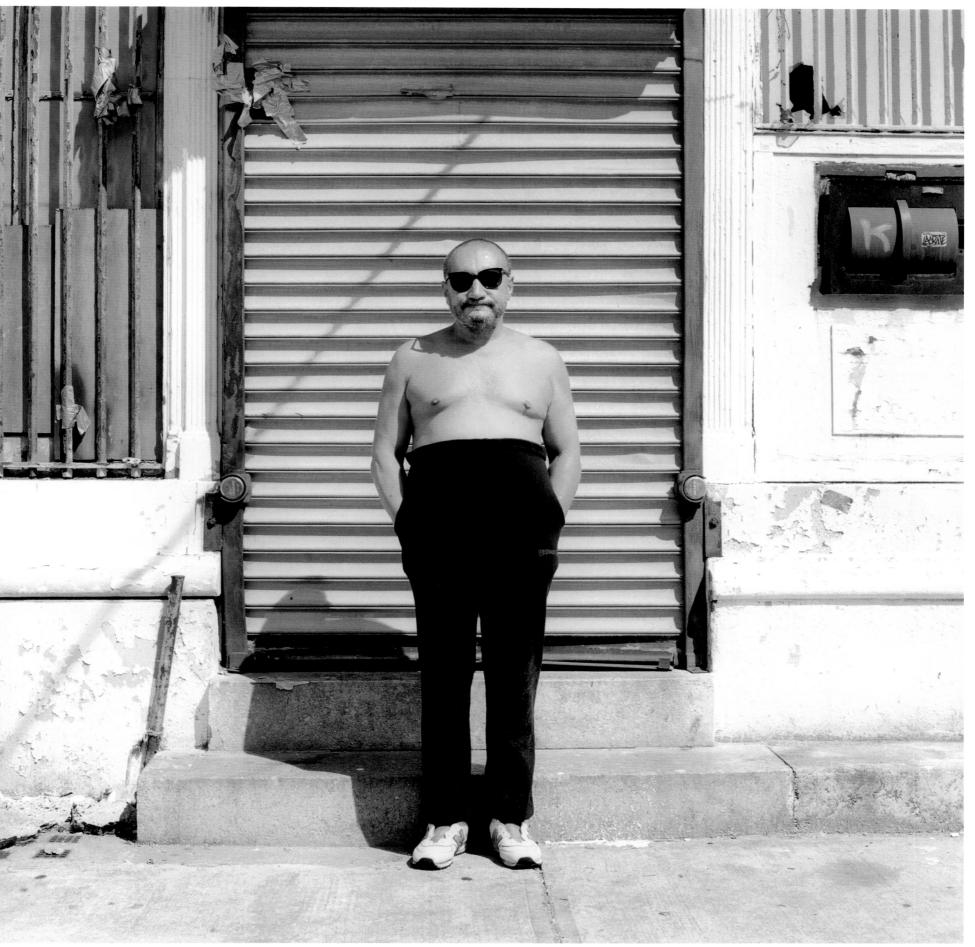

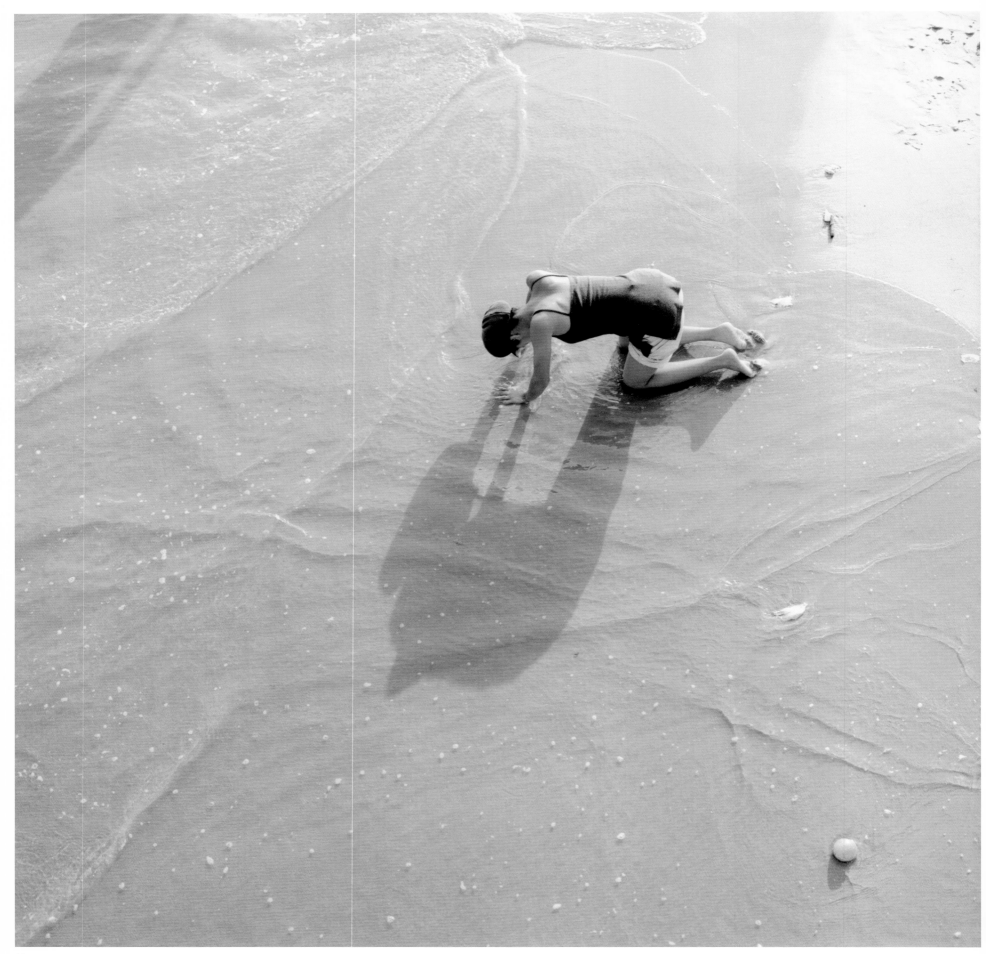

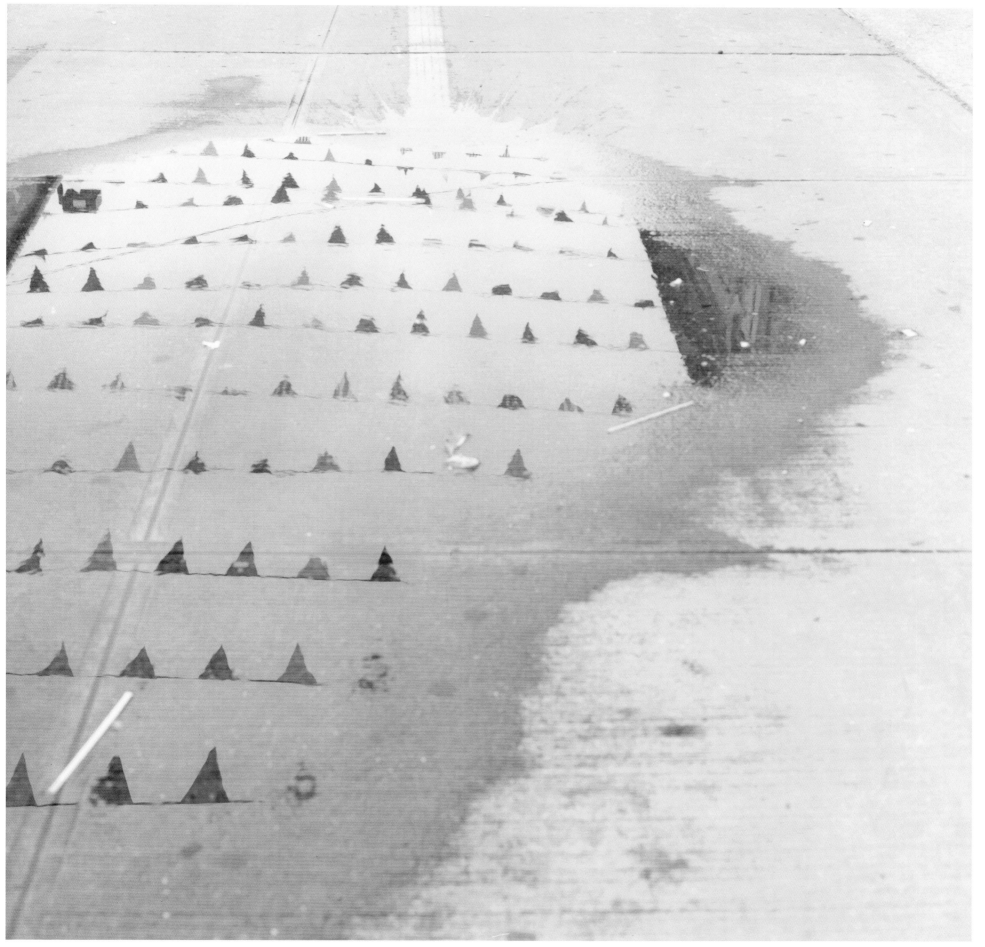

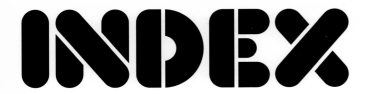

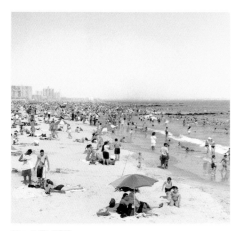

Beach 01, 2000
Page 22

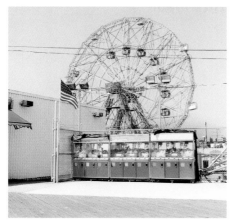

Wonder Wheel 01, 2002
Page 23

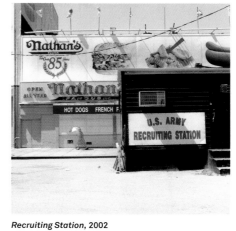

Recruiting Station, 2002
Page 24

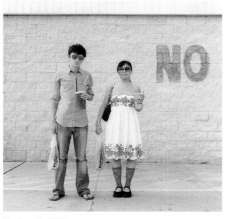

No Couple, 2003
Page 25

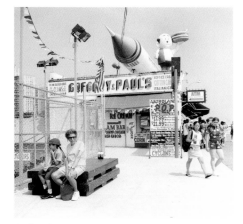

Rocket, 2003
Page 26

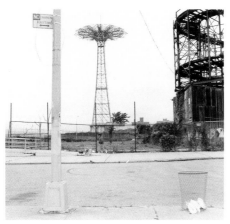

Parachute Jump, 2000
Page 27

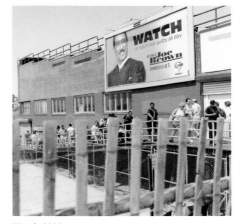

Watch, 2000
Page 28

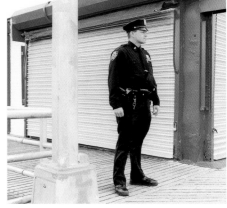

Cop, 2000
Page 29

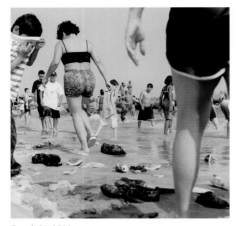

Beach 02, 2000
Page 30

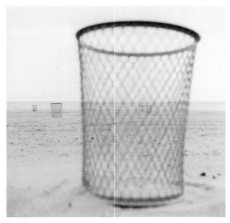

Trash Cans, 2002
Page 31

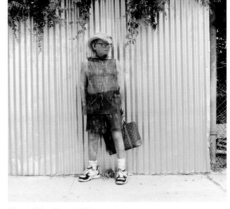

Man with a Bag, 2005
Page 32

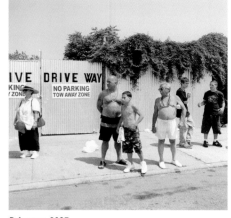

Driveway, 2005
Page 33

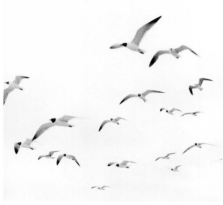

Seagulls, 2002
Page 34

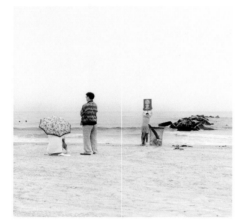

Beach 03, 2005
Page 35

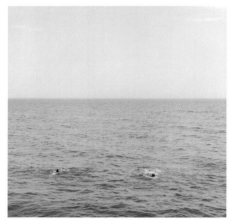

Two Swimmers, 2000
Page 36

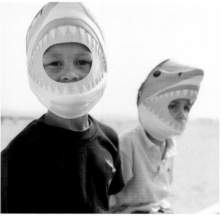

Shark Masks, 2000
Page 37

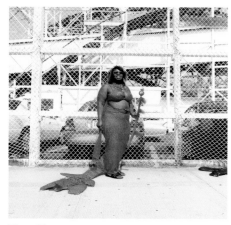

Mermaid 01, 2005
Page 38

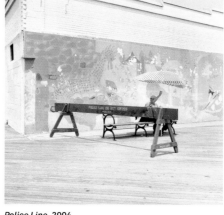

Police Line, 2004
Page 39

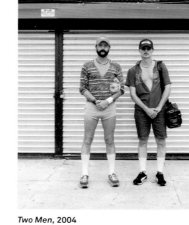

Two Men, 2004
Page 40

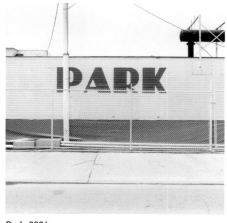

Park, 2004
Page 41

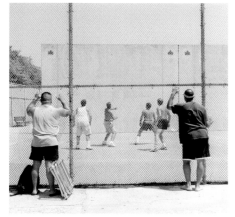

Fence 01, 2004
Page 42

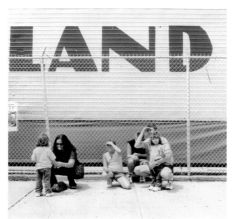

Family, 2004
Page 43

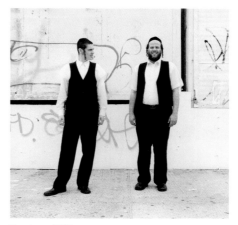

Two Jews, 2005
Page 44

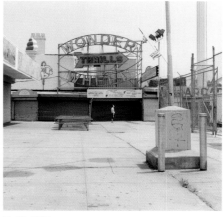

Thrills, 2004
Page 45

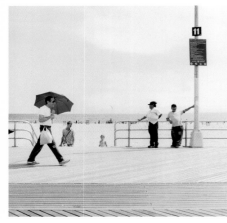

Boardwalk, 2004
Page 46

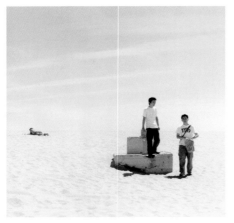

Beach 04, 2003
Page 47

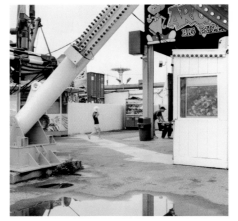

Big Prize, 2004
Page 48

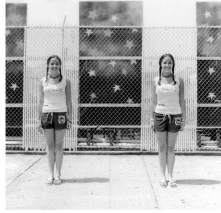

Twins, 2004
Page 49

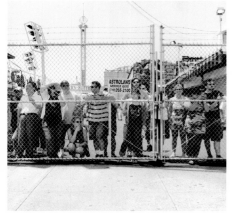

Fence 02, 2005
Page 50

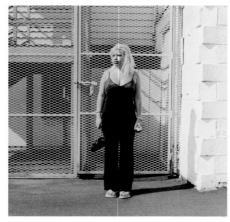

Woman with an Apple, 2005
Page 51

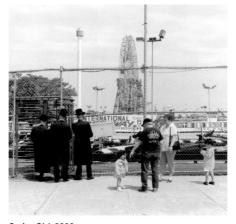

Crying Girl, 2000
Page 52

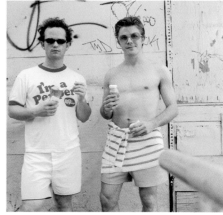

I'm a Pepper, 2000
Page 53

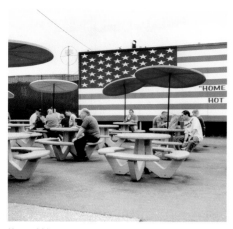

Home, 2004
Page 54

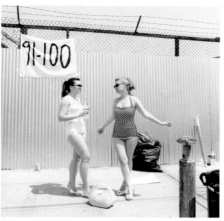

Two Girls, 2005
Page 55

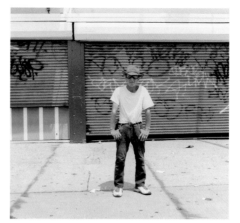

Man with Sunglasses 01, 2004
Page 56

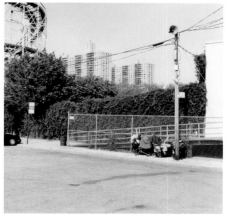

Belongings, 2002
Page 57

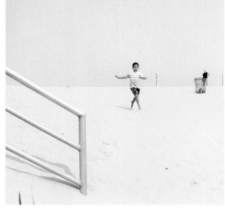

Beach 05, 2004
Page 58

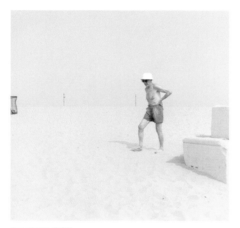

Beach 06, 2004
Page 59

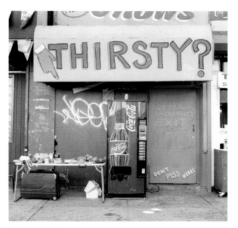

Thirsty, 2003
Page 60

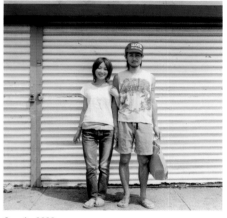

Couple, 2003
Page 61

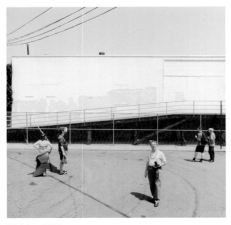

Waiting, 2005
Page 62

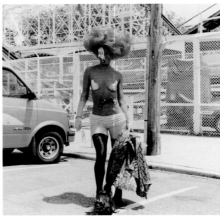

Mermaid 02, 2005
Page 63

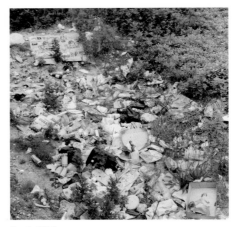

Trash, 2000
Page 64

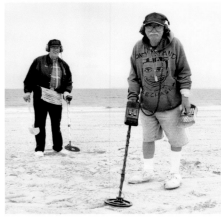

Treasure Hunters, 2000
Page 65

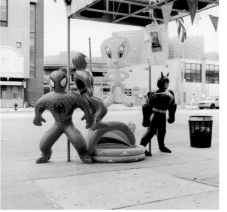

Heroes, 2005
Page 66

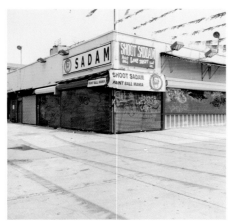

Shoot Sadam, 2004
Page 67

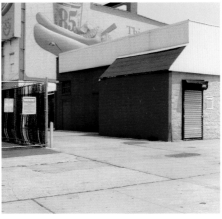

Hot Dog, 2004
Page 68

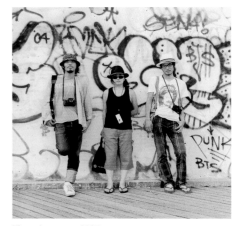

Three Japanese, 2005
Page 69

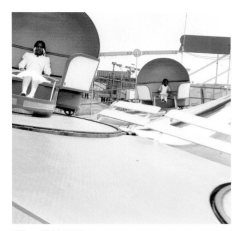

Tilt-a-Whirl, 2000

Page 70

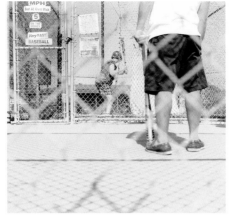

Very Fast Baseball, 2000

Page 71

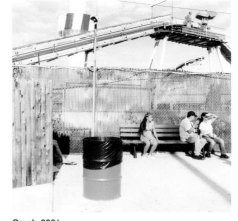

Break, 2004

Page 72

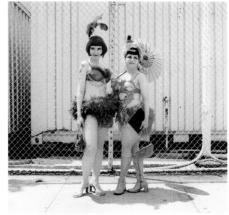

Two Girls in Costumes, 2005

Page 73

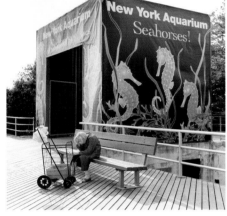

Old Lady, 2000

Page 74

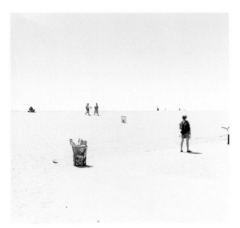

Beach 07, 2003

Page 75

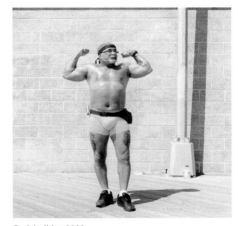

Bodybuilder, 2003

Page 76

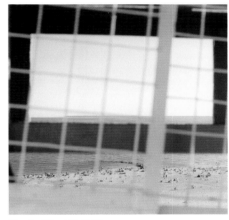

Wonder Wheel 02, 2003

Page 77

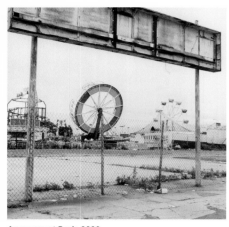

Amusement Park, 2000
Page 78

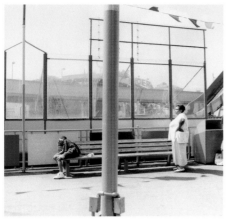

Woman and Boy, 2003
Page 79

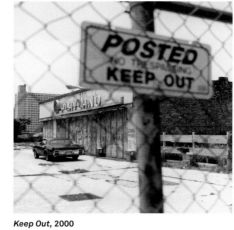

Keep Out, 2000
Page 80

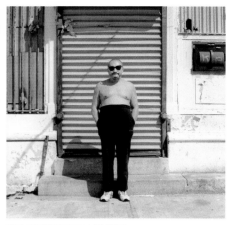

Man with Sunglasses 02, 2003
Page 81

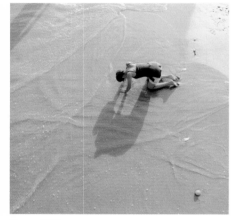

Prayer, 2000
Page 82

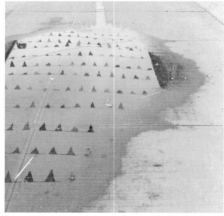

Reflection, 2002
Page 83

BIOGRAPHY

BIBLIOGRAPHY

ACKNOWL-
EDGMENTS

BIOGRAPHY
BIOGRAFIE

Curriculum Vitae
Lebenslauf

1971
Born in Hanover, Germany;
Austrian citizen

1991
First exposure to photography

2001
Admission into the
    World Press Photo Joop Swart
    Masterclass

2003
Admission into the
    German Academy of Photography (DFA)

2004
Membership in the
    artists' group POC Project
    (www.pocproject.com)

Awards
Preise

2006
Scholarship Kunststiftung
    Baden-Württemberg
Grants from the Landesbank
    Baden-Württemberg Foundation and
    the Federal Chancellery of Austria

2005
Two special mentions at the
    Hansel Mieth Prize
Honorable mention at the
    World Press Photo Awards

2004
Finalist at the
    Saar Ferngas Young Art 2004
Oskar Barnack Award
Grant from the Landesbank
    Baden-Württemberg Foundation

2003
Special mention at the
    European Architectural
    Photography Prize
Special mention at the
    International Prize for Young
    Photojournalism
Finalist at the
    Umbo Photography Award
German Photography Book Award
    for *Sun City*

2002
World Press Photo Awards, third place
Arles Discovery Award
German Social Award

2001
Special mention at the
    International Prize for Young
    Photojournalism

1997
Special mention at the
    International Prize for Young
    Photojournalism

Collections
Sammlungen

Fotomuseum Winterthur, Switzerland
Staatsgalerie Stuttgart—
  Grafische Sammlung, Germany
Fundación Ordóñez-Falcó, Spain
Landesbank Baden-Württemberg
  Art Collection, Stuttgart, Germany
Regional Council Stuttgart, Germany
Private collectors

Galleries
Galerien

Galerie Kamel Mennour, Paris, France
Hasted Hunt Gallery, New York, USA
Galeria La Fabrica, Madrid, Spain
14-1 Galerie, Stuttgart, Germany

Solo Exhibitions
Einzelausstellungen

2006
Kunsthalle Tübingen, Germany
Galerie Kamel Mennour, Paris, France

2005
Belfast Exposed, Belfast, Northern Ireland
Sala El Águila, Madrid, Spain
Centre culturel Les Chiroux, Liège, Belgium
Sala Amós Salvador, Logroño, Spain

2004
Galerie Kamel Mennour, Paris, France
14-1 Galerie, Stuttgart, Germany
Galerie 11, Hamburg, Germany

2003
Neue Börse, Frankfurt, Germany
Photo España, Madrid, Spain
Galerie photonet, Wiesbaden, Germany

2002
Fondazione Marangoni, Florence, Italy
14-1 Galerie, Stuttgart, Germany

2001
Galerie 11, Hamburg, Germany
Galerie photonet, Wiesbaden, Germany

1999
Junge Fotografie, Stadthaus Ulm, Germany
Rautenstrauch-Joest-Museum, Cologne, Germany

Group Exhibitions
Gruppenausstellungen

2005
Pingyao International Photography Festival, China
Backlight Festival, Tampere, Finland
14-1 Galerie, Stuttgart, Germany
Museum für Photographie, Burghausen, Germany
Estivales Photographiques du Trégor—
  L'Imagerie, Lannion, France
Internationale Fototage,
  Mannheim/Ludwigshafen, Germany
Galerie Altes Rathaus Musberg, Germany

2004
Galerieschiff, Frankfurt /
  Kulturbahnhof Eller, Düsseldorf, Germany
KAZ Kunstbahnhof, Kassel, Germany
Saarland Museum, Saarbrücken, Germany
TUFA, Trier, Germany
Kunstverein Ludwigshafen, Germany
Dialekt Festival, Stuttgart, Germany
Forum für Fotografie, Cologne, Germany
Rencontres d'Arles, Germany

2003
International Prize for Young Photojournalism,
  travelling exhibition, Germany
Bundeskunsthalle, Bonn, Germany
Stadtmuseum Oldenburg, Germany
Städische Galerie Lippstadt/Westfalen, Germany
Galerie l'Usine, Brussels, Belgium

2002
Oude Kerk, Amsterdam, The Netherlands
Visual Gallery of Photokina, Cologne, Germany
Galerie Maximilian Krips, Cologne, Germany
World Press Photo Exhibition, shown worldwide
14-1 Galerie, Stuttgart, Germany
Galerie Lichtblick, Cologne, Germany

2001
International Prize for Young Photojournalism,
  travelling exhibition, Germany
Netherlands-Foto-Institut (NFI), Rotterdam,
  The Netherlands

2000
Fotografie Forum International, Frankfurt, Germany

1999
Kunsthalle Bremen, Germany

BIBLIOGRAPHY
BIBLIOGRAFIE

Books
Buchveröffentlichungen

2006
Coney Island,
published by Hatje Cantz, Germany

2005
Alzheimer,
published by Kehrer, Germany

2003
Sun City,
published by Benteli, Switzerland

1997
Butlerschule,
published by Römerturm, Germany

Catalogues
Katalogveröffentlichungen

2005
World Press Photo
Centre culturel Les Chiroux, Belgium
Internationale Fototage Mannheim + Brückenprojekt
Backlight Festival, Finland
Pingyao International Photography Festival, China
Schrumpfende Städte

2004
Saar Förderpreis für junge Kunst

2003
Photo España
Internationaler Preis für jungen Bildjournalismus
Umbo Fotopreis
Europäischer Architektur Fotopreis

2002
World Press Photo

2001
World Press Joop Swart Masterclass
Internationaler Preis für jungen Bildjournalismus

1997
Peter Granser—Photographs
Internationaler Preis für jungen Bildjournalismus

ACKNOWLEDGMENTS
DANK

This book is dedicated to the people I met at Coney Island. They make this place very special.

For their energetic and valuable support in planning and realizing both this book and the exhibitions, I would like to especially thank Martin Hellmold (Kunsthalle Tübingen), Markus Hartmann (Hatje Cantz), Kamel Mennour (Galerie Mennour), Jörg Walz and Christine Michler (14-1 Galerie), Vicki Goldberg, Sabine Kunz (Stiftung LBBW), as well as Maik Stapelberg and Daniel Fritz (stapelberg&fritz).

Thanks are also due to my beloved Beatrice for her patience, advice, and great help in conceiving this project as well as in choosing the images for the book and the exhibition.

Peter Granser

Gewidmet ist dieses Buch den Menschen, die ich in Coney Island getroffen habe. Sie machen diesen Ort zu etwas Besonderem.

Für die tatkräftige und wertvolle Unterstützung bei der Planung und Realisierung des Buches und der Ausstellungen möchte ich mich des Weiteren ganz herzlich bei Martin Hellmold (Kunsthalle Tübingen), Markus Hartmann (Hatje Cantz), Kamel Mennour (Galerie Mennour), Jörg Walz und Christine Michler (14-1 Galerie), Vicki Goldberg, Sabine Kunz (Stiftung LBBW) sowie Maik Stapelberg und Daniel Fritz (stapelberg&fritz) bedanken.

Meiner geliebten Beatrice danke ich für ihre Geduld, ihren Rat und ihre große Hilfe bei der Entstehung dieses Projektes sowie bei der Bildauswahl für dieses Buch und die Ausstellung.

Peter Granser

Kindly supported by
Mit freundlicher Unterstützung von

Stiftung
Landesbank Baden-Württemberg
LB≡BW

BUNDESKANZLERAMT ▪ KUNST

Prolab
Stuttgart

COLOPHON
IMPRESSUM

This catalogue is published in conjunction
with the exhibitions / Diese Publikation erscheint
anlässlich der Ausstellungen

Peter Granser
Fotoserien 2000–2005
Kunsthalle Tübingen
April 28–July 2, 2006

Peter Granser
Galerie Kamel Mennour
60, rue Mazarine
75006 Paris, France
November 15–December 30, 2006

Copyediting / Lektorat:
Sylvia Massow (German / Deutsch),
Rebecca van Dyck (English / Englisch)

Translations / Übersetzungen:
Karen Lauer (Vicki Goldberg),
John S. Southard (Martin Hellmold)

**Graphic design and typesetting /
Grafische Gestaltung und Satz:**
stapelberg&fritz, Stuttgart

Typeface / Schrift:
Akkurat Bold, Light
Kada

Paper / Papier:
Munken Print Extra, 150 g/m²
Galaxi Supermat, 200 g/m²

Binding / Buchbinderei:
Kunst- und Verlagsbuchbinderei, Leipzig

Reproductions and printing /
Reproduktionen und Gesamtherstellung:
Dr. Cantz'sche Druckerei, Ostfildern

© 2006 Hatje Cantz Verlag, Ostfildern

© 2006 for the essay by Vicki Goldberg:
the author / für den Essay von Vicki Goldberg
bei der Autorin

© 2006 for the reproduced works by
Peter Granser: the artist / für die abgebildeten
Werke von Peter Granser beim Künstler

**A special Collector's Edition is available.
Please contact Hatje Cantz for more information. /
Es erscheint eine Collector's Edition.
Nähere Informationen erhalten Sie beim Verlag.**

Published by / Erschienen im
Hatje Cantz Verlag
Zeppelinstraße 32
73760 Ostfildern
Germany / Deutschland
Tel. +49 711 4405-0
Fax +49 711 4405-220
www.hatjecantz.com

Hatje Cantz books are available
internationally at selected bookstores and from
the following distribution partners:

USA/North America – D.A.P.,
Distributed Art Publishers, New York,
www.artbook.com
UK – Art Books International, London,
www.art-bks.com
Australia – Tower Books, Frenchs Forest (Sydney),
towerbks@zipworld.com.au
France – Interart, Paris,
commercial@interart.fr
Belgium – Exhibitions International, Leuven,
www.exhibitionsinternational.be
Switzerland – Scheidegger, Affoltern am Albis,
scheidegger@ava.ch
For Asia, Japan, South America, and Africa,
as well as for general questions, please contact
Hatje Cantz directly at sales@hatjecantz.de,
or visit our homepage www.hatjecantz.com for
further information.

**ISBN-10: 3-7757-1776-5
ISBN-13: 978-3-7757-1776-2
Printed in Germany**

**A French edition is available /
Eine französische Ausgabe ist erhältlich:**
Kamel Mennour / Paris Musées
ISBN: 2-914171-24-2
EAN: 9782914171243

Cover illustrations / Umschlagabbildungen:
Thrills, 2004
Beach 07, 2003